THE GREAT SKYSCRAPERS OF THE WORLD

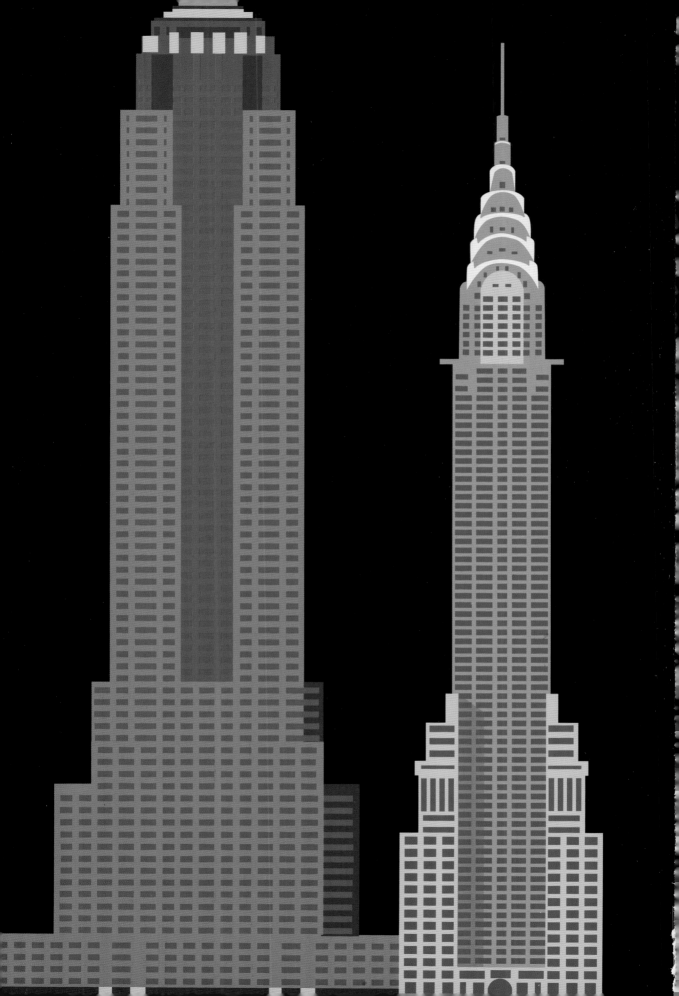

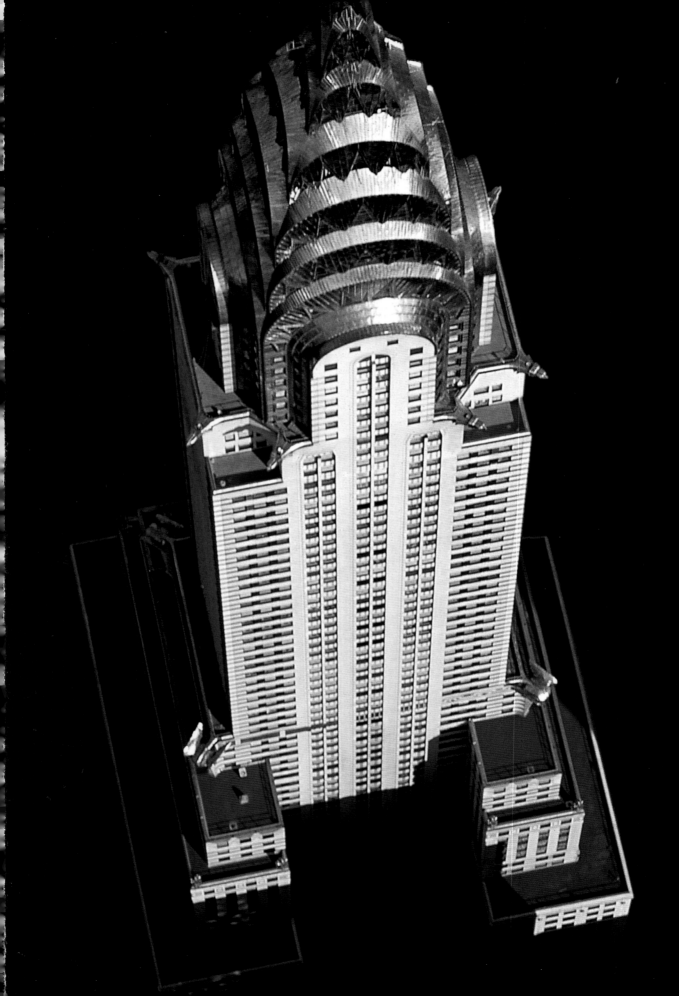

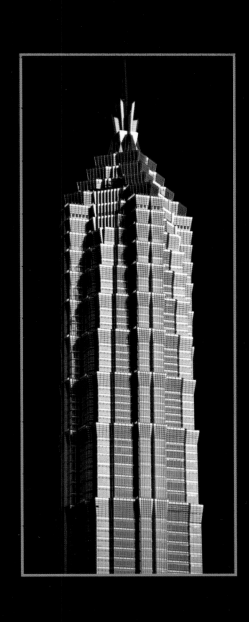

CONTENTS

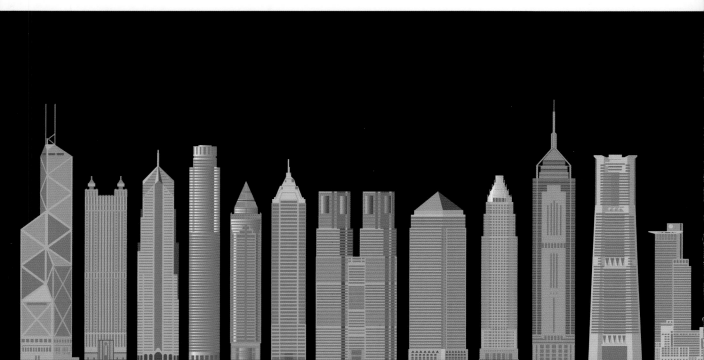

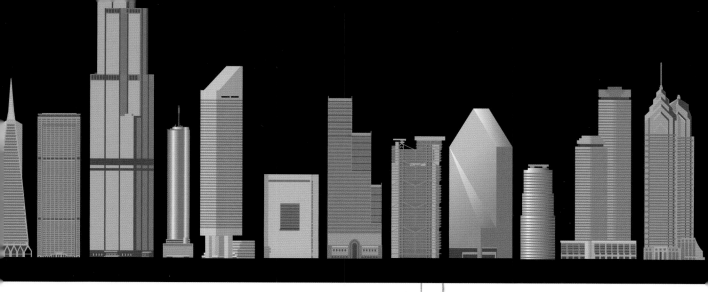

AUTHOR
Antonino Terranova

Editor
Valeria Manferto De Fabianis

Collaborating Editors
Maria Valeria Urbani Grecchi
Giada Francia
Alberto Bertolazzi

Graphic Designer
Clara Zanotti

Translation
Timothy Stroud

© 2003 White Star S.r.l.
Via C. Sassone, 22/24
13100 Vercelli, Italy
www.whitestar.it

ISBN 88-540-0000-0

REPRINTS:
1 2 3 4 5 6   07 06 05 04 03

Printed in Italy Rotolito Lombarda, Milan
Color separation by Fotomec, Torino

INTRODUCTION

1 ■ The Jin Mao Tower, 1,381 feet high, is the new symbol of Shanghai.

3 ■ The Bank of China skyscraper is the tallest building in Hong Kong at 1,211 feet.

4-5 ■ This famous photograph immortalized workers on a break during the construction of the Empire State Building.

5 right ■ The Empire State Building was the tallest building in the world for 40 years.

INTRODUCTION

7 ■ The Chrysler Building, built at the end of the 1920s, has an unmistakable style. Its esthetics were inspired by contemporary automobile design.

....

INTRODUCTION

After 2000 years of western architecture, the skyscraper suddenly appeared during the second half of the nineteenth century. As an architectural "type" it grew out of a compulsion that is as old as the world itself: to build as high as possible, touch the clouds, and reach the celestial world of the divine. Compared to previous buildings, the innovations introduced in the nineteenth century were the products of changing economic and social conditions and, above all, related to technology and city development. The result, however, also went toward satisfying an internal and ever-present need: to symbolically represent power.

To explain the skyscrapers of yesterday and today, this volume discusses them in their chronological order. This approach makes it easier to understand the transformations and discontinuities in this completely new form of construction. The playful skyline of the "singular objects" in Shanghai, for example, has nothing in common with the serial and vertical skyline of New York. The differences have seemed to increase in recent years, though interpretation of these differences is a difficult task. It is not known how skyscrapers will develop in the future, despite seeing them in light of how they have developed to date.

Before the nineteenth century, only a very few large monuments exceeded standard city buildings. The domes of Santa Maria del Fiore in Florence, St. Peter's in Rome, St. Paul's in London, and the towers of Notre Dame in Paris and Westminster Abbey in London threw symbolic shadows over their cities. They protected their inhabitants but never approached the heights of skyscrapers. These modern constructions – the offspring of unbridled capitalism, scientific and technological progress, and the concentration of commerce and business in city centers – are symbols of the people's aspirations, for which their architects have often had recourse to an iconography that dates back to ancient or biblical mythology.

The Tower of Babel has always represented the archetype of man's dream to build up to the sky: a dangerous wish accompanied by the risk of failure. Unsurprisingly, Babylon has always represented the notion of great cities as places of corruption that lure individuals away from godliness and naturalness toward decadence and collapse. Immensity tends to destroy a sense of limitations but it is in this that the attraction to the superhuman lies. This explains why skyscrapers should not seem to be the work of man but of an anonymous and superior entity.

In addition to mythological and biblical influences on the evolution of architecture, there are many others from all phases of history. The bell- and watchtowers of civil buildings, cathedral bell-towers, and the domes and spires of buildings of all religions are also archetypes of tower skyscrapers. Analogously, the profiles of turreted cities in medieval Europe – for example, the famous San Gimignano – were the true forerunners of modern skylines.

The imagination of the architects of skyscrapers has always had the gigantism of history's masterpieces to draw on: the pyramids and the Sphinx in Giza, the Colossus of Rhodes, and the Lighthouse of Alexandria were all constructions that still astonish for the uniqueness of their forms and their extraordinary size. Later, Christian cathedrals and Islamic mosques were considered paragons of beauty and size for centuries, to the point that the skyscraper was defined "the cathedral of the twentieth century."

8 ■ Toward the end of the nineteenth century, Frank J. Sprague, one of the inventors of the electric elevator, helped to eliminate the need to climb stairs on foot, thus allowing higher buildings to be designed.

....

9 ■ The Tribune Tower was built in 1925 in Chicago. If the Flatiron building in New York was considered simply a high-rise building, then this was the first true skyscraper and its design inspired many others in the years that followed.

....

Two of the wonders of the modern world that preceded sky-scrapers were the great lay monuments of the Eiffel Tower and the Statue of Liberty. The first was for many years the world's tallest structure until it was exceeded by the Chrysler Building. The second was associated with the Great Giants of New York as one of the most widespread icons of contemporary urban architecture, and was obliged to helplessly watch the events of September 11, 2001. Architects found another reference in nature, drawing inspiration from particularly uneven mountain ranges and canyons. Hence, in Manhattan Broadway can be referred to as "the gorge." According to Vitruvius, the architect Dinocrates offered to sculpt Mt. Athos for Alexander the Great into the shape of the seated emperor, with rivers and cities in his lap and the capital Alexandria in his left hand. Similarly, Mount Rushmore was carved with the faces of four presidents of the United States. Moreover, the tallest skyscrapers – at over 1,300 feet from street level – evoke man-made Enchanted Mountains. The works of nature, man, mythology, and religion have contributed to creating a "substrate of consciousness" in which the seed was planted that grew into the modern skyscraper, and when it came into being, its innovativeness compared to its forerunners became immediately apparent. The concept of the sky-scraper first saw the light in Chicago during the second half of the nineteenth century. During those years, the Windy City on the Great Lakes grew into a huge commercial crossroads for the Midwest. The expansion of the city's population went hand in hand with the increase in specialization of the central district, which was transformed into a city of offices, particularly company headquarters. The number of employees in large companies grew, thus requiring more space. When demographic and economic pressure increased with the construction of the Loop (the public aboveground rail transport system), the value of land in the city center with permission to build sharply increased. Like Lisbon after the earthquake or London after the Great Fire, catastrophe is often the impetus for a revolution in city development. In Chicago, the cause was the Big Fire of 1871, which razed the old city to the ground, thus creating space for new development. The ideas that contributed to the rebirth of Chicago had to take the requirements of an overly congested city into account and were given an exceptional stage in 1922 during the competition for the offices of the Chicago Tribune. The winning design was, in the years that followed, to represent in American architecture the predominance of the titanic, historicist, and late-Romantic collective imagination over the functionalist rationalism prevalent in Europe. In 1925, the Decorative Arts Exhibition in Paris led to the diffusion of a new synthetic and evolutionary vocabulary – Art Deco – that had a great influence on the appearance of skyscrapers. Equally significant in encouraging architects to look upward were important technical innovations achieved during the second half of the nineteenth century. The first related to the skeleton and sheath of a building, i.e., a load-bearing framework of steel girders and pillars over which a relatively independent wall of panels and glass was installed. This fairly resistant type of structure allowed buildings to be much higher than traditional constructions made using stone, brick, and wood, and allowed much wider spans between pillars. This permitted greater flexibility in the use of the open space created and still forms the basis of modern office buildings. The second innovation was the invention of the elevator, which did away with the need to climb stairs and thus made the height of a building irrelevant to its occupants; in fact, it gave greater value to higher buildings. Whereas the "aristocratic" floor of traditional European residences was the second, with the invention of the elevator the moneyed and management classes could move to the highest floors, closer to the sky and the light.

Up there, inside designs that often took the forms of symbolic spires, High Society and the Powers that Be began to move in, whether they were part of the management aristocracies of large automobile, broadcasting, banking, insurance, or financial corporations. The third innovation came with advances made in ventilation, air conditioning, and lighting systems that permitted the creation and regulation of a microclimate regardless of outside weather conditions. These breakthroughs meant that there was less need during the design stage to ensure "natural" light and ventilation. The essence of a skyscraper lies in its physical configuration. Louis Sullivan, one of the leading figures in the Chicago School, identified as one of the peculiar characteristics of a skyscraper the absolute coherence between the disproportion of its vertical

to its horizontal dimensions (and to the horizontal dimensions found in traditional city architecture). The Flatiron Building, built in New York in 1902, is 285 feet high, more than double the height of traditional buildings. However, its gigantism was furthered because it respected the classical three-part division derived from architectural orders, in particular from those of the ancient column: the "base" is formed by the first or lowest floors; the "shaft" is represented by the main floors with their identical rows of windows; and the "crown" of the building comprises the topmost floors and the attic, with larger windows and a large cornice to match the scale of the entire building. The Flatiron was a perfect example of the high-rise building, that is to say a vertically oriented construction, and was to become the fulcrum of the business district. From

INTRODUCTION

20

10-11 ■ Without any visible safety gear, a worker concentrates on his work on the Empire State Building. To the right is the Chrysler Building.

Chicago, where early experimentation had produced little more than tall buildings rather than skyscrapers, leadership in the race for supremacy in the construction of iron and steel giants passed to the island of Manhattan. It was here that skyscrapers achieved their first spurt in height and symbolic popularity with a generation of buildings located in a neighborhood populated exclusively by towers in a permanent height competition. This was Skyscraper City. In just a few years, a range of new giants was built: the Chrysler Building (1930), the Empire State Building (1931), and Rockefeller Center (1933-40). The Chrysler exceeded the Eiffel Tower, thus taking the height record across the Atlantic to the United States. The second exceeded the Chrysler just a year later, and remained the world's tallest building for several decades,

becoming one of a group of icons that characterized the city and the Confederation: the Statue of Liberty, the three Giants, the "Stars and Stripes," and the Brooklyn Bridge. Rockefeller Center signaled a transformation in the design of the skyscraper and its relationship with the city by offering a multifunctional urban complex in a single unit. It centered on a series of public spaces in which offices were integrated harmoniously with recreational areas. In 1929, the Wall Street Crash led to years of economic depression that tended to view skyscrapers as giants with clay feet. The Empire State risked bankruptcy and was only saved by the number of tourists who flocked there for the views from the top. Yet, vertical construction in Manhattan was not halted even if the general American attitude had changed.

In 1932, Scott Fitzgerald wrote in the conclusion to his *Tales of the Jazz Age*, "Lonely and inexplicable as the sphinx, rose the Empire State Building. I went to the roof of the last and most magnificent of towers. Then I understood... Full of arrogant pride the New Yorker had climbed here and seen with dismay what he had never suspected, that the city was not the endless succession of canyons that he had supposed, but that it had limits; from the tallest structure he saw for the first time that it disappeared into the country that, alone, was unlimited." The future of the skyscraper was already the future of the unbounded planetary metropolis. The construction of the Giants in New York occurred at the same time as the production of several movies that were to remain embedded in the Western subconscious. *Metropolis* by Fritz Lang described the conflict between the prince of the city, who lived at the top of the skyscraper palace, and the masses, who inhabited the underground tunnels of the city-factory. Lang deliberately used settings that echoed the forms of the Chrysler Building in a sort of Art Deco style blended with a machine-based Utopian Futurism. The reality of the city continued with the construction of high-rise buildings but only of medium height; this was the typology of building that conformed to building regulations. Skyscraper City consisted of skyscrapers, tall buildings, and high-rises, but also a huge distribution of ordinary, and even deteriorating constructions. New York, considered the first American and last European city, was the setting for another great urban transformation that was destined to spread worldwide.

12 and 13 ■ Directed by Fritz Lang, the movie *Metropolis* admirably reproduced the feeling of the social, economic, and urban revolution of the 1920s and 30s. Lang imagined a futuristic city in Art-Deco style in which continual conflict existed between the wealthy middle-classes, who lived at the top of the skyscrapers, and the working classes, forced to live underground.

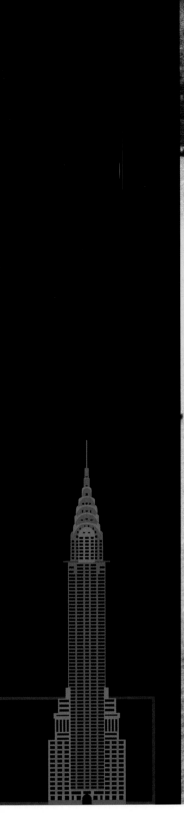

Whereas the south tip of Manhattan saw the growth of the financial center on Wall Street, despite the brake applied by the presence of the docks, the area immediately below Central Park, where Grand Central Station is located, became a midtown area bristling with skyscrapers. It was here most of all that construction boomed based on building regulations that governed overall height, and which therefore encouraged a diversification of building forms. The results included giant high-rises, apartment blocks with towers, buildings with successive setbacks in "ziggurat" style, and the box-shaped "plaza" skyscraper. The 1950s were a time of varying and sometimes conflicting tendencies. On the one hand there arose the more visionary and Utopian design, described in Ayn Rand's novel *The Fountain-*

head, built around the heroic figure of Frank Lloyd Wright, a modern, individualist, and rebel architect. In 1956, he envisioned a skyscraper a mile high in the creation of a low-density city named Broadacre City to counter the large, compact, and congested city. On the other hand, Mies van der Rohe and Philip Johnson, champions of the International Style, designed the Seagram Building in Manhattan in 1958. This was the prototype for and a masterpiece of the serial development of the box-shaped sky-scraper featuring a curtain-wall made of glass and steel. Van der Rohe and Johnson perfected experiments already undertaken in Chicago with the Lake Shore Drive Apartments by Van der Rohe himself and in New York with Lever House by the firm of Skidmore, Owens, and Merrill (SOM). The esthetic dimen-

14-15 ∎ In the 1930s, Manhattan was "skyscraper city." Vertical expansion occurred thanks to building regulations that encouraged great heights.

sion of repetition and precision was used, and it was only later that it became trivialized in the anonymity of standardized multinational architecture. The birth of the "plaza" was another novelty of the Seagram Building: provided that the pure parallelepiped was set back from the street, new building regulations allowed the skyscraper to increase in height without requiring the architectural steps back that had produced the ziggurat style. The resulting pedestrian space was outfitted with the first examples of "urban furniture."

The postwar period also saw the first skyscrapers built outside the United States. In Europe, numerous obstacles slowed the rise in height of buildings, one of which was the growing importance placed on the safeguarding of historic cities and a certain degree of ideo-

logical suspicion that branded "American-style" tall buildings as monuments to capitalism. Various ways were suggested to acclimatize cities to the arrival of skyscrapers. In Paris, bitter controversy accompanied the proposal for construction of the Montparnasse Tower and the urban renovation that it entailed such that authorities decided to move the office and skyscraper district into peripheral areas like La Défense. In Milan, the Pirelli Building was built with carefully drawn and sculpted forms as an object of modern design, whereas the Torre Velasca incorporated traditional turreted figures that evoked the city's historical identity. Moscow attempted to constrain the individualist anarchy of skyscraper design within a schematic and hierarchic city development plan.

17 ■ **The World Trade Center's Twin Towers**
represented the close relationship between
the skyscraper and the financial power. Even
before the 9/11 attack, they had lost their
crown as the world's tallest building to the
Sears Tower in Chicago.

The 1960s marked the rebellion of late-Modern architects against the use of repetition with a slew of bizarre forms like the first "Twins" in Marina City (Chicago, 1962), the pointed Transamerica Pyramid (San Francisco, 1972), the truncated pyramid of the John Hancock Center in which the diagonal strengtheners were visible from the outside (Chicago, 1969), and the Twin Towers of the World Trade Center (New York, 1972) that were immediately recognizable owing to the concept of duality. The Twin Towers became the tallest buildings in the world and were almost a sculptural work of land art.

Their story is one of expectation and hard-fought promotion and construction. To build these artifacts, their financiers, including the billionaire Rockefeller, had to cut their way through the tangle of city development regulations governing Manhattan. The architect Minoru Yamasaki was obliged to produce dozens of variations before the final one was accepted. As the height of buildings grew, the World Trade Center doubled in size with the creation of a twin tower for reasons of esthetics and economy of scale. Since the 1970s there have been further developments in the form and function of skyscrapers, in their artistic expressiveness, in the functions they offer the city, and in their image as portrayed by the media.

The design of the Citicorp skyscraper (New York, 1977) opened the building' bottom floors to create a semi-public space for commerce and entertainment. The John Hancock Tower (Boston, 1976) is famous for its glass paneling that reflects the historic monuments surrounding it.

The Sears Tower (Chicago, 1974) returned the height record to the Windy City thanks to the innovative use of groups of "tubes" in the structure that produce an inimitable vertical figure. The image of the turreted skyline was by now widespread, serving to identify that part of the city that started to be called "downtown." Andy Warhol's film *Empire* and Woody Allen's *Manhattan* presented Skyscraper City at all hours of the day, emphasizing its titanic qualities.

With the advent of the 1980s, there was a reaction to late-Modern designs, which graduated into post-Modernism. In this style, architects began to make physical references to and reinterpret models of skyscrapers from the heroic age. Contemporaneously, the high-tech aesthetic began to gain ground, leading to the construction of a number of buildings marked by excess. Remarkable stylistic contrasts began to be seen in the same city, as in Frankfurt with the Messeturm (1990) and Commerzbank (1997) buildings.

The presence of skyscrapers in both the United States and Europe was becoming one of the major factors in the urban renewal of important but often neglected districts. Outstanding examples are the renovation of Times Square in New York, the conversion project for the Docklands in London – culminating in the construction of the Canary Wharf Tower in 1991 –, and the restoration of the area around Alexanderplatz in Berlin.

19 ■ At 1,483 feet tall, the Petronas Towers in Kuala Lumpur hold the current record for height, which they won from the Sears Tower in Chicago in 1997.

20-21 ■ This inventive photomontage of 1945 shows a man pedaling across a tightrope stretched between New York's two symbols: the Empire State and Chrysler buildings.

During the last twenty years of the twentieth century, having begun as early as the 1970s, the phenomenon of skyscrapers spread outside the West. The Overseas Chinese Bank (Singapore, 1980), the National Commercial Bank (Jeddah, 1983), and the Hong Kong & Shanghai Bank (Hong Kong, 1990) are examples. In the East, the rush to build upward became frantic in the late-1990s. Skyscrapers became representative of geopolitical transformations and sprouted at an extraordinary rate in uninhibited, bizarre, and original designs. The shift of the world height record from the United States to Malaysia – from the old Twin Towers to the new Petronas Twin Towers and from the ambiguous purity of two parallelepipeds to the non-Western historicism of what has been called the "technological pagoda" – was emblematic. The formation of the planetary metropolis records the prevalence of the Pacific over the Atlantic and more generally the growth in importance of Asia. The historic model of the skyscraper was reproduced in the hotel New York, New York in Las Vegas. Downtown became a "historic center" to all intents and purposes and was looked after with constant development programs; new skyscrapers, like the Condé Nast Building, were deconstructed so that they could be more easily absorbed into their settings. Even cinema made the shift across the ocean when the film *Entrapment* used the Petronas Towers as its setting much like *King Kong* had used the Empire State Building and, in its remake, the Twin Towers of the World Trade Center. As suggested in a recent photographic exhibition called "Not So Far East," East Asian interpretations of the cosmopolitan architectural patrimony seems to have created synthetic and surreal imitations of things already seen. Simulations, imitations, and clones of existing buildings seem to be creating a supranational, but vaguely mysterious, metropolis, partly because these derivations maintain subtle Chinese, Japanese, and Malaysian nuances. In Europe, the most common model is the post-Modern clone of historic Western architecture invested with Gothic, Art Deco, or Modernist characteristics, whereas in the East there is an abundance of original figures in terms of both new typologies and hybrid vocabularies that have resulted in eccentric designs. Skyscrapers in the form of "bamboo shoots" blend high-tech and organic elements, as seen in the Menara Telecom Tower in Kuala Lumpur. In Dubai, there is a seven-star hotel in the form of a sailboat in the middle of the desert. The Jin Mao in Shanghai is a new, gigantic technological pagoda. In the East, skyscrapers in the shape of a great canopy that create covered public spaces, analogous to the Grande Arche in Paris, confront bridge, gateway, and urban-chamber themes rather than the eternal motif of the skyscraper as tower. However, they tend to using a high-tech language that seems to hark back to the intergalactic sterile atmosphere of *2001: A Space Odyssey*. That is the case with the Umeda Sky Building (Osaka, 1993) and the NEC Super Tower (Tokyo, 1990). The advent of the new millennium was celebrated with massive projects but was also marked by the destruction of the Twin Towers. The disconcerting discovery of skyscrapers' fragility does not seem, however, to have slowed their evolution. The challenge has been accepted, starting from the many projects drawn up for New York's Ground Zero. The new models use biocompatible high technology, like the Swiss Re Tower in London, or they make use of naturalistic metaphors or esoteric philosophies in "singular objects" plunked down in metropolitan settings. Such destructured, globalized ideas as these have led to the plans for the world's highest skyscraper to stand in Shanghai's already extraordinary skyline. The skyscraper was the world's final architectural expression in what the famous historian Eric J. Hobsbawm called the "century of extremes" or "the era of great cataclysms." He presumed that the century had finished with the fall of the Berlin Wall, but unfortunately, that was not the final collapse. Despite the warnings of the prophets of the "end of history," history continues, and skyscrapers, with their many extravagant and varied forms, promise to continue to be the strangest and most marvelous of "Metropolitan Monsters."

Flatiron Building

Flatiron Building

Manhattan's oldest high-rise is also one of its most famous. The Flatiron gets its nickname from its triangular shape, the result of the designer's brilliant response to its location at the crossing of Fifth Avenue and Broadway, as the latter is one of the very few avenues in Manhattan's grid of streets and avenues that runs diagonally. It is one of the most recognizable landmarks in the city skyline.

Its plan – like that of other buildings such as the Times Tower by Eidlitz and MacKenzie, and the Equitable Building by Ernest Graham – is marked by the maximum 'lengthening' that the building could tolerate while still retaining Louis Sullivan's Chicago School "residential building" model. The school soon moved on to the "bell-tower" model, the most famous example of which is the 1913 Woolworth Building, designed by Cass Gilbert. Because of the presence of a frame-like structure permitting additional floors, the residential model could not be heightened further, on the contrary to the bell-tower model in which the building itself would be slightly lower but a crowning, recognizable element could be placed on top of it in the form of a bell-tower.

The Flatiron was originally known as the Fuller Building after its promoter George Fuller. It was designed by Daniel

22 ■ The front view of the Flatiron Building makes it possible to appreciate its main characteristic: an isosceles-triangular form with a beveled angle that gives it the appearance of a giant column standing in the middle of midtown Manhattan.

23 ■ The horizontal division of the façade is another unmistakable trait of the Flatiron. The elements placed on the crown of the building, like the large projecting cornice and an order of gigantic ashlars, evoke the decorations on Renaissance palaces.

24 top left ▪ The design sketches of the elevations demonstrate an attempt to create harmonious proportions typical of classical architecture.

Location	Project	Height	Materials	Completion Date
New York (U.S.A.)	Daniel H. Burnham	285 ft.	Steel and terra cotta	1902

24 top right ▪ The Flatiron Building during construction. The steel frame was lined with terracotta and then decorated with classical-style elements.

25 ▪ The imposing structure of the Flatiron, located on the meeting of Fifth Avenue and Broadway, overlooks the busy streets. The businessman who commissioned the Flatiron Building, considered it to be the most powerful building ever built.

Burnham with John Wellborn Root in the Beaux-Arts style. This choice was criticized by many architects at the time and followed from the fact that the architect had organized the World Columbian Exposition in 1893 in which, rather than carry forward the modernist ideas typical of Chicago at the time, he chose Neo-Classicism, and thus caused, in Sullivan's words, "damage that was to last for half a century."

The Flatiron follows the model of Renaissance palazzos in that it has balanced proportions and a three-part façade divided into an ashlar base, a central body that contains many stories, and a crown composed of a penthouse with very high arches and cornices at the top. It is said that the building has a double personality: if seen from the side, the Flatiron looks like a residential building, but if viewed from the front, it resembles a column. Divided into a base, shaft, and crown, the rounding of the sharpened end of the building, just six feet six inches wide, furthers its antique image. The base was built with large apertures and ashlar blocks for the first three floors, anchoring the building to the ground, while the shaft has been given an image of lightness. The crown is decorated with arches, columns, and an elaborate cornice. The façade is lined with terra cotta and decorated in a Renaissance manner.

The Flatiron was one of the first buildings to be given a steel skeleton. Consequently, it could be built to a height of 285 feet. A mix of eclectic elements and historical decorations masks the heavy structure underneath.

Woolworth Building

Woolworth Building

he skyscraper has been called the modern-day cathedral; infact, the Woolworth Building was termed"the cathedral of commerce." Its promoter and inventor was Frank Woolworth, the man who revolutionized commerce by creating large-scale distribution. He founded, with some colleagues, the company that bears his name and which, by 1912, was worth $ 65 million. He was responsible for the construction of one of Manhattan's most famous buildings, which was also the highest until the appearance of the giants of the 1930s that raised the city's profile by 350 feet or so, thus overtaking the renowned Eiffel Tower. The Woolworth Building stands out in the last generation of high-rise constructions that resembled ordinary buildings. They stretched ever upwards and were increasingly embellished with decorative features typical of Eclecticism. During this first generation of high-rise buildings, architects made use of a historical, rhetorical, and monumental vocabulary that was paradoxical for buildings expressing a radical socio-economic innovation. The task of designing the building was given to Cass Gilbert, architect of the Eclectic, who in those years had, in addition to others, designed the Customs Building in Beaux-Arts style. For the Woolworths he chose Neo-Gothic, believing it to give the tower a greater sense of vertical thrust and aspiration.

26 ■ The Woolworth Building, one of Manhattan's most famous structures, still fascinates visitors with its perfect coordination of esthetics and functionality, not to mention its charming use of Gothic architectural themes.

27 ■ Like the large majority of Manhattan buildings, the Woolworth Building was planned to accommodate offices. Its U-shape layout was the most efficient way to allow natural light into the building's interior.

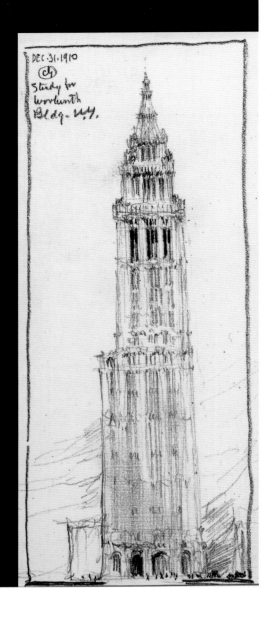

DEC. 31. 1910
Study for
Woolworth
Bldg - N.Y.

Study for Woolworth Bldg
at Watertown NY
DEC 6 - 1915.

Although it did not bear particularly innovative features compared to other buildings of the period – the Metropolitan Life Building by Napoleon Le Brun (1909) or the Singer Building by Ernest Flagg (1908) – the Woolworth became an example for many skyscrapers that were produced thereafter. With its 59 stories, it was the tallest building in the world from 1913 to 1930.

Situated on the corner of Broadway and Park Place in the banking district of Wall Street in downtown Manhattan – a zone where development was difficult due mainly to the presence of the port – the supporting structure is made of steel and is formed by a cage-like system of girders and columns. The tower consists of a 29-story building standing on a U-shaped plan from which emerges the so-called "bell-tower." The presence of the bell-tower, which would eventually form an actual architectural typology, became a feature typical to this first generation

28 top ■ The studio drawings best demonstrate the vertical aspirations behind designs for the Woolworth Building.

28 bottom ■ The photographs of the building's construction show how it was formed by a steel-cage skeleton of pillars and girders, later lined with Gothic-style elements evoking traditional themes.

29 ■ The Woolworth Building stands in downtown Manhattan and is still today one of the symbols in the city's skyline. Conceived as a monument to the commercial power of the Woolworths, it also represented the climax of Cass Gilbert's career: he earned much respect thanks to the project. Gilbert made great efforts to adapt a Gothic style to a modern, operational structure, creating a new style that was to influence many other buildings in the metropolis.

Location	Project	Height	Materials	Completion Date
New York (U.S.A.)	Cass Gilbert	791 ft.	Steel and terra cotta	1913

30 and 30-31 ■ The use of terracotta facing in the main structure of the Woolworth Building made it possible to easily reproduce decorative elements typical of Gothic style such as groin ribs, arches, spouts, and gargoyles.

WOOLWORTH Building

of skyscrapers. Atop a relatively traditional building accommodating the majority of the building's functions, a tower-like structure was added as a distinctive element that also allowed the edifice to reach a higher elevation.

The Woolworth differs from other bell-tower buildings in that there is no separation between the heavy base and slender tower; they are joined and thus contribute, along with the Gothic style, to giving the building an upward thrust that is further emphasized by the use of ribbing.

The reference to Gothic style is repeated in the series of arches, towers, and gargoyles. Even the cross-shaped atrium is covered by a vault supported by two-story arches and is completely decorated with mosaics, wrought iron, eclectic ornamentation, and precious materials. The bust of Cass Gilbert is also significant in that it holds a model of the Woolworth Building in its hands, an image recalling the iconography of a patron saint often found in ancient cathedrals. Similarly, the polychrome, terra-cotta-lined façade is also finely decorated with Gothic elements.

Chrysler Building

The Chrysler Building stands in Midtown Manhattan, at the intersection of 42nd Street and Lexington Avenue, just one block from Grand Central Terminal, the famous railway terminus built on the initiative of the railroad king, Cornelius Vanderbilt, who styled himself one of the "princes of the city." The facility was opened in 1913.

The skyscraper's highly distinctive profile begins with a base of three floors that covers the entire block; it then narrows through a series of progressive setbacks as it grows in height. The central section is composed of numerous stories on which sits a sort of cornice accentuated by eagle heads, after which it continues to rise and taper until it narrows to take on the shape of a spire or fastigium. Here, a number of themes are evident: the crown of the city, the shining sun of progress, automobile images, and futuristic representations typical of the 1940s in New York, with dirigibles that fly above the other skyscrapers in Midtown. The Chrysler was the first of the three giants to rise in New York between the 1920s and 30s due to a number of new circumstances that, paradoxically, arose during a time of crisis. Until the completion of the Empire State Building in 1931, it took the prize for the "the tallest building in the

Chrysler Building

32 ■ The Chrysler Building looks down on midtown Manhattan with its tapered silhouette and its shiny, extravagantly decorated spire, inspired by automobile designs.

33 ■ This famous photograph of a decorative eagle head modeled after a hood ornament of a Plymouth automobile portrays Margaret Bourke-White intent on photographing New York City from above.

world," thus stealing this distinction from the Eiffel Tower in Paris and transferring the symbol of progress from the Old World to the New. The three giants will always stand among the icons of Manhattan and among the tallest, but also most imaginative and wonderful, skyscrapers of the world. The Chrysler's iconic design and elegant, sharply etched representations have always earned it a first place among buildings for beauty tied to a certain "feminine" quality. It has also been defined as an "object" in that it was a product of "macro-design" (new to the period), which emphasized the creation of an architectural landmark or logo on both a metropolitan and planetary level. This is backed up by its regular presence in New York City's and the United States' heroic iconography, in advertising as well as films. The hard-fought competition to design the Chicago Tribune Building entered by important representatives of avant-garde European culture

Location	Project	Height	Materials	Completion Date
NEW YORK (U.S.A.)	WILLIAM VAN ALEN	1,047 FT.	STEEL, GLASS, BRICK, AND CHROME	1930

34 top ■ Walter Percy Chrysler, founder and president of the automobile company, followed his skyscraper project with great determination.

34 bottom left ■ A worker is photographed on steel scaffolding at the 54th floor during construction on the skyscraper.

34 bottom right ■ During construction the innovative structure of steel pillars and trusses is apparent.

35 ■ William Van Alen secretly assembled the spire but only installed it once construction of the Bank of Manhattan headquarters had been completed. It appeared at the top of the skyscraper as if by miracle, in one the most famous battles of "skyscraper war."

36 top ■ The interior spaces of the Chrysler Building are decorated with the same elegance as the exterior. On this ceiling, the building itself was painted, while elsewhere the century's innovative means of transportation were portrayed.

36 bottom ■ The display room, located in the ground floor and renovated in 1978, and the luxurious entrance hall richly decorated with steel, marble, and granite from around the world demonstrate how even the details of the building were chosen to be the best in the world.

37 ■ Conceived as a monument to the golden age of the automobile, the Chrysler Building has a unique design featuring references to car parts such as radiators, wheels, and bodywork decorations.

(such as Walter Gropius and Adolf Loos), clearly showed that the United States was in search of an image for itself that differed from Modernism. It also showed new paths for architects to follow in the design of American skyscrapers: extremely vertical orientation of the structure's walls; emphasis on architectural elements, decorations, and spires that harked back to Classical or Gothic images with a romantic twist; the taking-up of heroic stylistic features from bourgeois Eclecticism; images from non-European architecture such as Babylonian ziggurats or Aztec temples; and finally, the blending of all this with the monumental vocabulary of the Beaux-Arts, a staging of historical and architectural monumentality (revisited on a "superhuman" scale). It was only in the postwar period that International Style took the upper hand together with a new type of urban skyscraper, the stacked "glass prisms of the modern city."

Urban regulations had

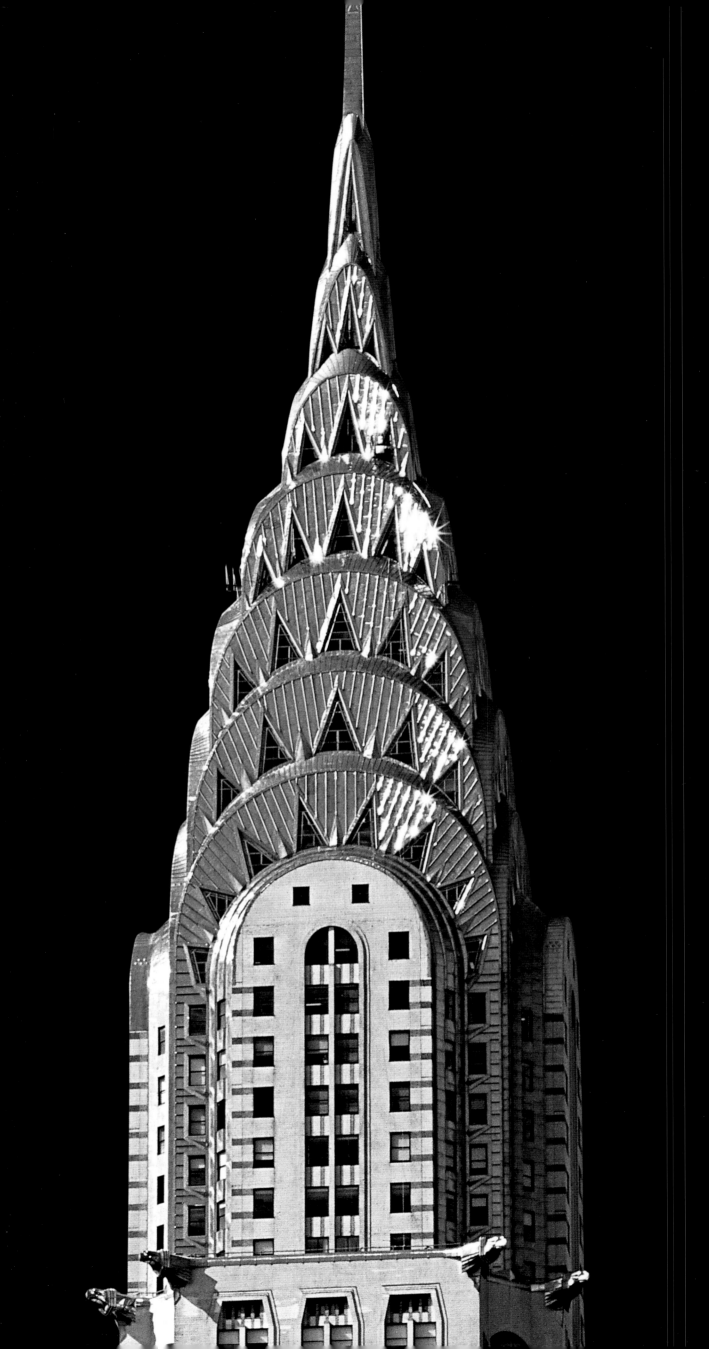

38-39 ■ The Chrysler Building's spire is its best-known and most important feature. Representing the shining sun of progress and created with references to the automobile, its function was to act as the crown of New York.

38 bottom ■ The credits in the film *Bonfire of the Vanities* scroll against a view of Manhattan with, in the foreground, eagles looking out toward the horizon. In fact, the eagles are none other than the steel decorations on the Chrysler Building, icons of the skyscraper and the city itself.

changed to protect the quality of the streets that were choked on all sides by high-rise buildings. With ever-increasing heights, it became necessary to encourage the construction of buildings whose upper floors retreated from the street while allowing them to rise as high as they liked at the center of the site. The tendency then moved toward increasing the size of the actual building lot to gain sufficient area for the central section. Thus, a new type of skyscraper evolved, one that became a fact of urban life as it vied to achieve the latest record in height. The structure of steel pillars and trusses cooperated with the central core (where the elevators were located) to re-

sist the horizontal force of the wind, leaving the façade facings free of all static functions.

New technology was also developed for the elevator systems, forced ventilation, central heating, acoustic isolation, the collection and elimination of waste, and other services. The materials used, carefully chosen for brightness and durability, were likewise important, such as the stainless steel used in the spires that boasted shiny surfaces and a long life.

According to some, the Chrysler represented the quintessence of this type of skyscraper, and yet, very shortly afterwards, the third giant of the city – Rockefeller Center – greatly distinguished itself with its variety of

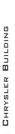

structures, having internal and external sections that together formed a multifunctional building that was more open to the city. More recently, the variants on the skyscraper have increased in number. The Utopian and gigantic vision that the new culture and new building regulations encouraged was explicitly expressed by Hugh Ferriss in his famous views of an ideal city, but also in comic strips and the cinema. A remarkable parallel could be seen in the great palace (the crown of which recalled the Statue of Liberty) in Fritz Lang's 1927 movie, *Metropolis*, which took two years to plan and produce. Metropolis is divided into an underground city for the workers and an "aerial" city of tall and imposing buildings, busy multi-level roads, and viaducts for pedestrians and vehicles on various levels.

The effects on employment of the Wall Street Crash in 1929 took decades to shake off but occurred when the numbers of automobiles produced were already falling to record levels. The automobile industry was fundamental to the American economy and had experienced its greatest boom when, during the first decade of the twentieth century, Henry Ford introduced his utilitarian vehicle for the masses, the Model T. In this depressed economy, Walter Chrysler built the skyscraper that bears the company's name. Just when the economic crisis was eroding profit margins across the automobile industry, Chrysler (who founded his automobile company in 1925 after having worked for the Union Pacific Railroad) decided to build a monument to the golden years of the automobile industry. This desire inspired the design of the building, which is decorated with motifs of car radiators, wheels, and other decorations, in particular, that year's Plymouth. Construction of the Empire

CHRYSLER Building

State Building, a private venture, began in 1929. The Empire State then held the record for the world's tallest building for thirty-odd years until David Rockefeller indefatigably promoted the World Trade Center, built by Port Authority of New York and New Jersey. An expedient used by William Van Alen — the Chrysler's architect — is linked to the "skyscraper war" that was taking place in New York during those years. Inside the topmost stories, he secretly prepared the construction of the spire but only put it into place, with extraordinary speed, once the headquarters of the Bank of Manhattan had been completed, designed by his rival H. Craig Severance. Another facet of the skyscraper war was a sort of curse that fell on the great architects: as had occurred to others, following scandals about the financial running of the company, Van Alen fell into disgrace and never recovered the same level

of glory he had known with the Chrysler. However, that did not stop him from participating in the Beaux-Arts Ball wearing a legendary costume resembling the Chrysler Building, with the spire on his head. He along with other of New York's most famous architects were photographed each dressed as one of their own designs. The Chrysler Company never moved its head offices into the building but just created a showroom on the ground floor. The building was renovated in 1978 with the construction of a welcoming and luxurious entrance hall richly decorated with steel, marble, and granite from all over the world. In 1995, the chrome spire — named "Nirosta" — was restored to be shinier than ever and particularly visible at night, as was the Empire State Building, which stands out owing to the splendor of the differently colored flood-lighting of the upper floors.

40 and 41 ■ In 1995, restoration of the chrome "Nirosta" spire was completed. The spire reflects external light and magnifies internal light, thus becoming a characteristic icon of New York both by day and by night.

Building

Empire State Building

The Empire State Building – the very icon of the skyscraper and what was long the tallest building in the world – celebrates itself in the central panel on a wall in its 100-foot-long, 3-story-high entrance hall. In this hagiographic portrayal, the Empire State is colored gold, radiates an aureole of divinity from its antenna at the top, and is ringed by medallions that illustrate the steps taken on the progress of humanity. The "center of the universe" and eighth wonder of the world, the Empire State does not hide having been purposely conceived to be the tallest building in the world. It won this record from the Chrysler Building in 1931 and held onto it until 1972 when the construction of the World Trade Center marked the start of a new era. After the destruction of the Twin Towers, the Empire State has reluctantly returned to being the symbol of New York and America. Its highly recognizable profile combines with extraordinary statistics relating to

42 ■ The symbolic power of the building lies most of all in its distribution of volumes. Starting from a base of five stories, a series of bodies rise that gradually step back until the central body extends like a telescope to the 86th floor. The construction continues to rise and taper until it forms the antenna.

43 top and bottom ■ The 1933 movie *King Kong* used the symbolic appearance of the Empire State Building as a setting. In the film, the tower and antenna, already planned as a berth for dirigibles, formed the backdrop for the allegory of Beauty and the Beast and the struggle between artifice and nature.

its construction to increase the building's appeal: 10 million bricks, a weight of 365,000 tons, 59,800 tons worth of steel girders, 429 miles of electric cable, and 2.4 million square yards of windows with a full-time team to clean them.

However, the most striking quality of this 1930s symbol of power lies in the massive and dynamic distribution of volumes that pulls the attention of the viewer upward. Starting from a base of five stories that covers an area of 1.6 acres, a series of bodies rise that gradually taper until the corner sections terminate and the central body extends like a telescope to the 86th floor. The construction, however, continues to rise and taper until it turns without interruption into the antenna.

The sensation of plasticity created by such a gigantic object strongly rooted to the ground, but equally thrusting toward the sky, is accentuated by the repetition of modular windows that are

Location	Project	Height	Materials	Completion Date
New York (U.S.A.)	Shreve, Lamb and Harmon	1,250 ft.	Steel, brick, aluminum, and limestone	1931

44 ■ The Empire State Building during construction. Note the steel frame lined with brick and aluminum panels and other stone materials

45 ■ The façade is characterized by the endless repetition of modular windows grouped horizontally but also aligned vertically to highlight the vertical bands of empty and filled spaces.

46 and 47 ■ Workers pose daringly in the typically "adventurous" and pioneering attitudes associated with construction work on skyscrapers. The Empire State used prefabrication techniques, which greatly shortened construction time.

grouped horizontally but, above all, aligned vertically to create a triumph of empty and filled spaces and an immediately apparent ornamental motif.

The forms of the Empire State Building are closely linked to Art Deco but reveal an unexpectedly rich backdrop of ideas than one might not expect. First of all, there is the triumphal, but also somewhat threatening, Biblical image of the Tower of Babel; then, references to the movies and comics of the era such as the fantastic structures in Fritz Lang's *Metropolis* or the comic strip *Flash Gordon*; and finally, the visionary drawings of the future of the American city by Hugh Ferriss.

It is important to recognize that the extreme verticality of the Empire State is the result of the transformation of building regulations in Manhattan. As the buildings grew ever higher, to reconcile the rights of individuals to build on their land with the rights of others not to be disturbed by excessive elevations, two types of construction were encouraged, depending on the

area being built on. The first promoted progressive set-backs from the façade that produced a forest of ziggurat-style skyscrapers while the second, in which the central portion of the building site could theoretically proceed as high as it liked, resulted in a number of skyscrapers with central towers or bell-towers that replaced the old high-rise, "vertically-developed" buildings.

The Empire State Building, along with the Seagram Building, is a landmark in Midtown New York, just as the Twin Towers were a landmark in Downtown, from all of which superb views could be had over the city itself and the surrounding region.

48 and 49 ■ After a slow start, the Empire State Building became one of the preferred points from which to admire the city's panorama. Since the 1940s about two million tourists a year have ridden up to its observation deck to enjoy the breathtaking view.

50 ■ On the central panel of its charming entrance hall, the Empire State Building is portrayed in gold, radiating an aureole of divinity and sovereignty.

51 ■ The skyscraper, with its dizzying heights, represented the era's optimistic attitude about the future, then challenged by the Great Depression. The top is illuminated with colored lights on special occasions and important holidays.

The Empire State owed its initial success to the latter quality. In the years following its inauguration, its owners found it difficult to find companies willing to rent the office space, to the point that the new tower came to be known as the Empty State Building. Fortunately, the observation terraces held impending bankruptcy off by quickly becoming a tourist attraction that has since been visited by millions of people. Considering that the construction and inauguration of the building fell during the period of the Wall Street Crash and the subsequent Depression, from which America emerged only after World War Two, making a success of the Empire State was an enormous challenge.

Even though from a financial point of view it was not the best investment, as a symbol of America it enjoyed a worldwide triumph. Hollywood did not delay in exploiting it, and made use of its interiors, terraces, and views to draw spectators, for example, in *King Kong* (filmed in 1933 when construction had only just been completed), *On The Town* (1949), *Empire* (directed by Andy Warhol in 1964) and *Manhattan* (directed by Woody Allen in 1979). Its roles in these films were always central: as a gymnasium for a giant athletic gorilla, as a backdrop to a love story, as a stage for an experimental theater of the absurd, and as a supporting actor in the skyline of the Vertical City.

The Empire State is so famous that it has practically become humanized in the imagination

52-53 ■ The Empire State is one of the main landmarks of New York City. At night, the light filtering from its 6,500 windows continues to draw attention to this global symbol and constant presence in the collective imagination.

of New Yorkers and certain bizarre artists. The drawings by M. Vriesendorp hyperbolize the characteristics of skyscrapers and ironically endow them with human features. In the most famous, Rockefeller Center opens a bedroom door to surprisingly find a virile Empire State and the elegantly feminine Chrysler Building in bed. The bedside rug is designed in the form of the street layout of Manhattan and the Statue of Liberty is the nightlight; outside the window, other skyscrapers are glimpsed looking in curiously.

Designed to capture attention rather than meet particular building needs, the Empire State has been more successful than other skyscrapers of its age in the role of flying the flag and being a symbol of the American Dream. It has been recreated in innumerable gadgets, featured in advertisements, and been grouped with the Chrysler Building, Rockefeller Center, and the Statue of Liberty to raise — on a planetary level —the skyscraper to the level of an icon. The presence in the relatively new city of Las Vegas of a sort of model of the New York skyline signals the triumph, diffusion, and, perhaps, the decline of a model created to symbolize the Empire State (the State of New York) and that has continued until today to represent the paradoxical vertical spiritualism of the financial power of capitalism. Indispensable to the collective conscience of a city and a nation accustomed to economic crises but impermeable to them, the Empire State continues in its transcendental job of pointing out not only the sky to new generations of Americans but also any new challenges to overcome in the Third Millennium.

Rockefeller Center

Rockefeller Center

Rockefeller Center was the third of the giant buildings to appear in Manhattan during the years of the Wall Street Crash and its aftermath. Whereas the Chrysler and Empire State buildings vied for supremacy as the tallest building in the world, the great innovation of Rockefeller Center lay in its dimensions and layout. The aim was not to create a single building but a part of the city that covered three blocks, from Fifth to Sixth Avenues and from 48th to 50th Streets, offering different functions and opportunities for people to gather and be entertained in locations that were joined by pedestrian walkways.

The project began in 1926 when it was decided to build the Metropolitan Opera, to be designed by Benjamin Wistar Morris, but it was not possible to find a suitable location as prices in the central areas of Manhattan were too high for the construction of an auditorium. In 1928, Morris found an area of three blocks belonging to Columbia University on which he started work on his definitive design. It was typically Beaux-Arts in style, which dictated that the building had to be a symbolic and fantastic object set upon a symmetrical foundation. His plan called for a monumental design, flanked by two skyscrapers, and topped by the Opera itself. Once he presented the design, John Rockefeller, the billionaire founder of Standard Oil,

54 ■ Unattached to the structure beneath, the façade of the RCA Building, the heart of Rockefeller Center in New York, is characterized by a uniform, surface lined with basic materials. This choice seems to have been made more for economic reasons than esthetic ones.

55 ■ The construction of the imposing Rockefeller Center complex, which occupies a large area within the city, was possible thanks to its promoters' clever exploitation of advantageous conditions created in the aftermath of the Great Depression.

56 left ■ The drawings show the complex distribution of the volumes of Rockefeller Center. It is composed of a series of buildings of different heights that narrow toward the top.

56 bottom ■ Two of the artists that worked on the complex's decorations, Mexico's Diego Rivera (left) and Spain's Jose Maria Sert, compare notes.

56-57 ■ The use of a cage structure, innovative for that period.

was interested in financing it but invited a number of other architects to add commercial areas and offices to the design to make it more marketable. In 1929, the American economy was at its lowest ebb, but the architects continued to work, attempting to imbue the project with an idealistic and symbolic value more than simply commercial. In 1931, 14 structures were built and, by 1940, Rockefeller Center provided a workplace to more than 225,000 people. Between 1957 and 1973, the number of buildings increased to 19. In 1932, Radio City Music Hall, whose performances and broadcasts have since become a New York institution, was inaugurated.

The final design includes five office towers, a taller central building,

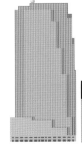

Location	Project	Height	Materials	Completion Date
New York (U.S.A.)	Reinhardt & Hofmeister, Corbet, Harrison & MacMurray, Hood, Godley & Fouilhoux	850 ft.	Steel and Limestone	1933

WISDOM AND KNOWLEDGE SHALL BE THE STABILITY OF THY TIMES

30

58-59 ■ The entrance to the General Electric Building – the largest in the complex – is decorated in Beaux-Arts style.

59 top right ■ The decorations enlivening the walls were inspired by heroic and mythological themes, often taking the form of divinities symbolizing various virtues or figures concentrating on their work.

59 bottom ■ Lee Latrie's bas-relief *Wisdom* stands out among the ornamental features on the façade of the central entrance.

and four buildings at the corners of the rectangle that covers three blocks. At street level, there is Rockefeller Plaza, Radio City Music Hall, and other theaters. There is also a sunken piazza onto which shops and cafés face that, in winter, is turned into a skating rink; the main axis of the piazza terminates in the entrance to a subway station.

Perhaps because it was designed by a committee and for the events that occurred during its construction, Rockefeller Center brought together different trends and met different needs. The Beaux-Arts background of many of its architects resulted in an attempt to confer a linear look and monumentality on its design, as demonstrated by the style of its decoration (Paul Manship's *Prometheus* – the symbol of progress – is displayed on the central axis of the building above the entrance, and Diego Rivera's mural stands in the entrance hall). The need to increase the economic value of the buildings meant building them tall and incorporating remunerative func-

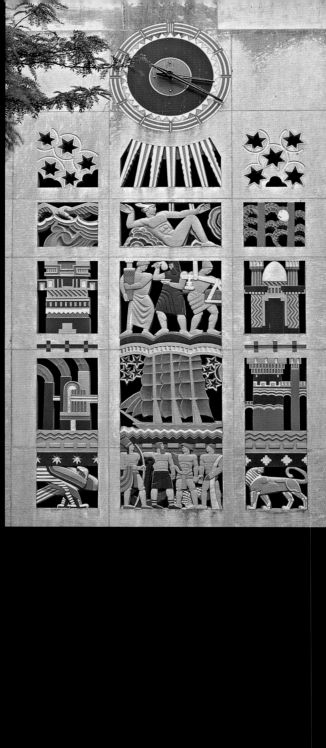

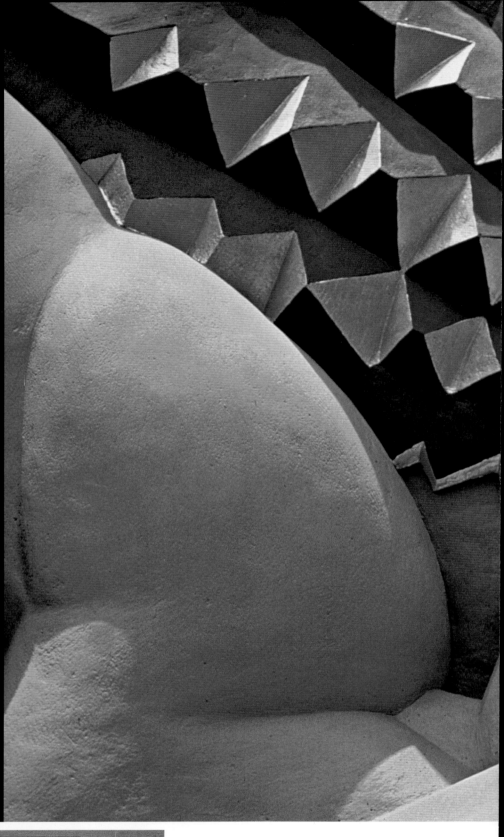

60-61 ■ The bas-relief over the side entrance to the General Electric Building was created by Lee Latrie. All the decorative work is typified by grandiosity and a certain pomp largely expressed by the use of expensive materials and the color gold.

60 bottom and 61 bottom ■ In addition to the many architects who worked on the Rockefeller Center, 30 artists were invited to decorate the façades, entrances, and gardens, including Paul Manship, Diego Rivera, and Lee Latrie.

62-63 and 63 bottom ■ The most characteristic element of the complex is the sunken piazza reached through Channel Gardens. The Gardens contain flowers and pools and lie on the same axis as the façade of the main building. Paul Manship's famous statue *Prometheus* dominates the area.

63 top right ■ Classical themes, seen mostly in the statuary elements, pervade the decorations in the plaza.

64-65 ■ The piazza is a public park area that in winter is transformed into a skating rink. Every Christmas, a large tree is installed above the gilded statue of Prometheus opposite the entrance to the plaza and decorated with elaborate lighting.

tions. Finally, the attempt to create environmental well-being with light, air, and greenery was provided by hanging gardens on the roofs of the lower buildings. When viewed from above, these gardens give a view of nature that must have been influenced by ideas of the Hanging Gardens of Babylon, the modernist Ville Radieuse (Radiant City) by Corbusier, and Elio Saarinen's never-realized design for Chicago Station. Moreover, the importance of Rockefeller Center lies in its use of a cage-like structure in which pillars are connected by horizontal trusses to absorb the loads, leaving the façade restriction-free. The façade is formed by a sand-colored limestone curtain-wall that retreats as it rises. With the return to popularity during those years of Gothic tastes, Rockefeller Center was designed with "buttresses" that, given the building's height, seem no more than slender ribbons. By terracing the towers, external balconies were created that allow more natural light into the offices not to mention neighboring buildings.

Moscow University

At a time when the rest of the world was experimenting with new building techniques using steel, at the end of the Second World War Stalin had seven skyscrapers built in eclectic Beaux-Arts style as symbols of military victory and an expression of the totalitarianism of his power. The skyscrapers were part of a reconstruction program for the city based on a plan approved in 1947 in which the strategic placement of the new buildings in certain parts of the city was designed to stimulate the development of the neighborhoods around them, the vertical element serving as a point of reference. Though commonly called skyscrapers, these Moscow buildings are not standard in that typically skyscrapers are usually independent of the city fabric surrounding them. The seven buildings are similar in appearance and style though the complex of Lomonosov University is unquestionably the most grandiose. At a height of 787 feet, it was the tallest building outside the United States at the time of its construction. The group of buildings was erected in an area that was previously occupied only by vegetable gardens and on which many buildings as well as a botanical

66 ■ The symmetrical layout of the main building is placed in relation to the central axis so that the perspective ends in the ascending element of the tower.

67 top ■ The monumentality of the building is expressed in the main façade by the tower and 187-foot spire topped by a star decorated with ears of wheat.

67 bottom ■ The park at the foot of the building is also laid out symmetrically in relation to the central axis that develops into the monumental Glory Avenue.

68-69 ■ The Great Hall can seat up to 1,500 people.

69 bottom ■ This is a view of the gym where artistic gymnastics are practiced. It is one of many facilities that contribute to making the university a city within a city.

garden, a stadium, and a park were subsequently constructed. The University is based on a set of dislocated buildings symmetrically laid out around a central axis. This continues and develops into Glory Avenue, lined with statues of Russia's greatest scientists, creating a principal perspective that ends in the ascendancy of the tower. The monumentality of the building is reflected in each of its elements including the tower, which is topped by a spire 187 feet tall and crowned by a star decorated with ears of wheat, and two lateral wings each 18 stories high that slope down to arms of eight stories each. These, in turn, are crowned by a clock, a barometer, and a thermometer. Access to the building is given through a portico of massive columns that support a trabeation decorated with bas-reliefs. Lastly, access to the entire group of buildings is given through a large square that lies on the main axis. The square features fountains, gardens, and a terrace that is an extraordinary viewpoint over the whole of Moscow. The entire façade of the building is decorated and embellished with statues. Those that attract the most attention are Vera Muchina's statue of two students at the en-

Location	Project	Height	Materials	Completion Date
Moscow (Russian Federation)	L. Rudev, S. Cernysev, P. Abrosimov, A. Chrjakov	787 ft.	Reinforced concrete and glass	1953

trance and N. Tomski's monument dedicated to Mikhail V. Lomonosov in the internal court. The University in its entirety covers 412 acres and includes a large 1500-seat hall, 6,000 student rooms, a student club, 19 conference rooms, 140 classrooms, numerous scientific laboratories, an agronomy museum, a library, a swimming pool, and various gymnasiums. The university is not just the center of the district but also one of the most important reference points in the Moscow skyline. It bears witness to a phase of society that continues to conceive of central power as an elevated concept.

Pirelli Building

onstruction of the Pirelli building began in 1956 during a period of economic boom. It was commissioned by the Pirelli Company to be its head offices, but today it is the headquarters of the Regional Council of Lombardy. At 417 feet tall, it was one of the highest buildings in Europe at the time. It became the symbol of Milan for its pure form, elegance, and visibility from every point in the city.

It is the most important and best known skyscraper in Italy, much more so that the others built shortly thereafter such as Velasca Tower in Milan, the Piacentini and Vega skyscrapers in Genoa, the Tange office building in Bologna (built in the 1970s), and the Tange office building in Naples (completed in the 1990s). Since the 1930s, Giò Ponti had given Rationalism his own interpretation, but he switched to Internationalism after World War II. He therefore wanted to design an "expressive," "isolated" building uninfluenced by surrounding constructions, roads, or the lot on which it was built. It had to be pure and belong more to the world of Italian Style than follow the dictates of architecture.

On the other hand, the Velasca Tower, built in Milan in 1958 by the BBPR Group, was not planned to be sculptural, out of scale, or impose its character on the urban landscape. Instead, it was designed to take figurative elements from the

70 ■ A main feature of the façade is its visible structural elements. The two triangular lateral pylons and the two central pillars taper toward the top to create a greater sense of verticality.

71 ■ The 417-foot-tall Pirelli skyscraper, besides being one of the tallest buildings in reinforced concrete in the world, is one of the most elegant structures thanks to its rounded sides.

Grattacielo
Pirelli
(1955-60)

Arch. G. Ponti A. Fornaroli
A. Rosselli G. Valtolina
E. Dell' Orto

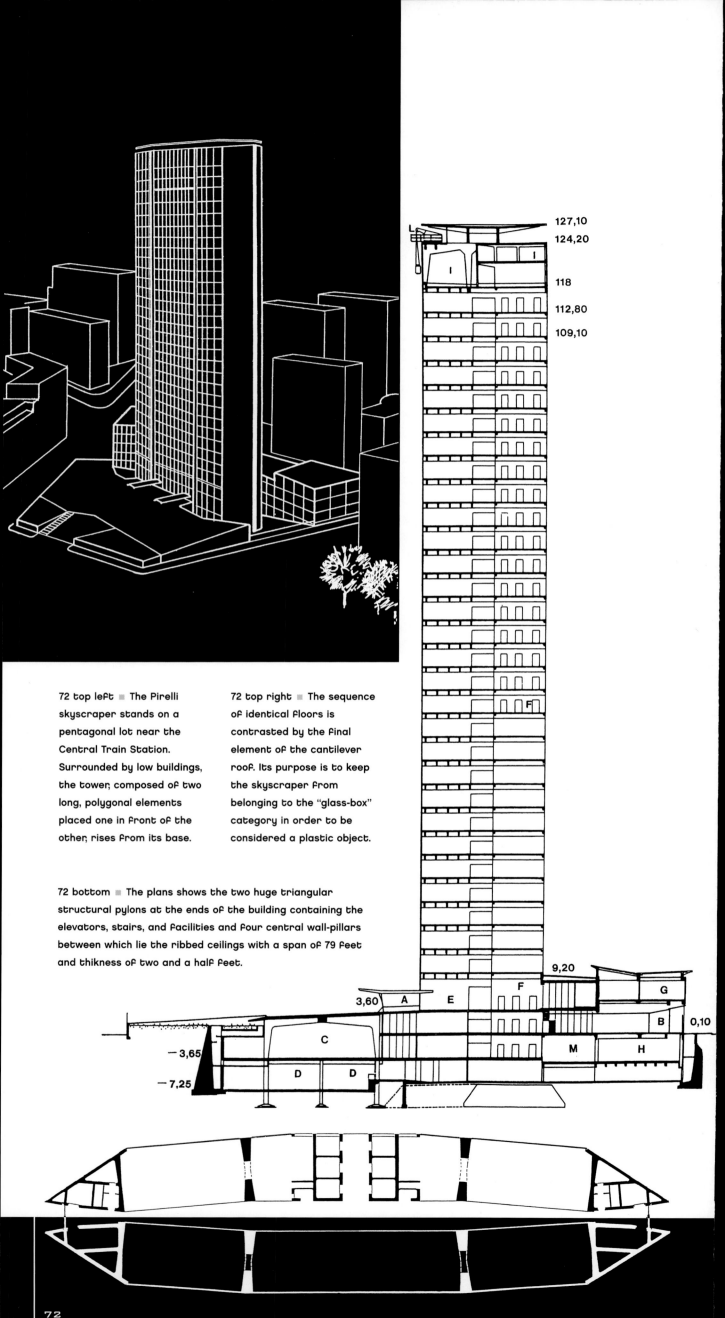

72 top left ■ The Pirelli skyscraper stands on a pentagonal lot near the Central Train Station. Surrounded by low buildings, the tower, composed of two long, polygonal elements placed one in front of the other, rises from its base.

72 top right ■ The sequence of identical floors is contrasted by the final element of the cantilever roof. Its purpose is to keep the skyscraper from belonging to the "glass-box" category in order to be considered a plastic object.

72 bottom ■ The plans shows the two huge triangular structural pylons at the ends of the building containing the elevators, stairs, and facilities and four central wall-pillars between which lie the ribbed ceilings with a span of 79 feet and thikness of two and a half feet.

127,10
124,20
118
112,80
109,10

9,20
3,60
0,10
A E F G
B
C M H
—3,65 D D
—7,25

73 ■ Milan has long been recognizable thanks to the Pirelli skyscraper overlooking Piazza Duca d'Aosta. The building, the fruit of the most intensely productive years of the architect Giò Ponti, represents a sort of secular tower that blends well into the Italian architectural tradition.

Location	Project	Height	Materials	Completion date
Milan (Italy)	Giò Ponti	417 ft.	Reinforced concrete and glass	1958

city and its history and create a dialectical relationship with it. It was therefore designed in the form of a medieval tower featuring many characteristics of traditional buildings. The Pirelli building, on the contrary, was designed with a curtain-wall to hide tectonics and construction and to be like a crystal pointing up into the sky.

In contrast to what has been said above, a sort of Classicism confers a strong degree of linearity on the structure, further characterizing this building. It is oriented parallel to Piazza Duca d'Aosta on which it stands and opposite Milan central railway station, in line with its main entrance. The main entrance opens onto the square, thereby determining the internal layout of the building. The secondary façade lies on the other side where the maintenance facilities are located. The tower stands on a pentagonal lot and is surrounded by a base (containing the conference rooms, the auditorium, the dining room, etc.) enclosed by low buildings in which the building's air-conditioning systems and other facilities are installed. Above them, two inclined bridges contribute to the tower's tall and slender appearance.

The plan is formed by two reflected polygonal elements set beside one another and measures 231 feet long by a maximum of 61 feet wide. The reduced width of the building means that the requirement

for artificial lighting, to which every skyscraper has to resort, here does not exist, as natural light reaches every point inside the building. However, the restricted width causes significant structural problems, the resolution of which was entrusted to Pier Luigi Nervi, one of the most famous engineers of the twentieth century. Nervi himself described it as follows, "the fundamental structural characteristic exists in the concentration of floor loads on the smallest possible number of load-bearing structures."

The structure is formed by two large pillars, triangular at either end, which contain the facilities equipment and distribution elements, and four central wall pillars, between which lie the ribbed floors with a span of 79 feet and thickness of two and a half feet. The entire structure was made thinner by the reduction in loads: the floors were tapered toward the exterior and the pillars toward the top in order to reduce the thickness at the front and so as not to impede the vertical thrust of the building. The restricted number of structural elements and the presence of wall-pillars gave great freedom of internal distribution. This was based on a 37-inch module, which provided a square grid and allowed spaces to be created that could subsequently be modified. In 2002, the structure withstood the crash of a small tourist airplane into the 24th and 25th floors.

Marina City

The importance of the two towers of Marina City, built by Bertrand Goldberg, is that they are an example of a multifunctional complex situated in the center of the city. This was a popular theme in the 1960s resulting from the fear that sections of a city composed purely of office buildings would be deserted in the evenings and weekends. The Marina City towers are 587 feet high (at the time of construction they were the tallest buildings to be built in reinforced concrete) and consist of an embedded base containing public spaces and a port for mooring boats on the river, 19 stories of parking lot for 896 automobiles with a spiral ramp, and, from the 20th to 60th stories, residences and offices. The structure is based on a static core in which a huge central column measuring 32 feet in diameter contains the facilities and distribution systems (five elevators and an emergency stairway) and forms the backbone of the tower. Being central, it is able to absorb the horizontal strain of the façade as transmitted by the floors. Fifteen pillars are arranged in a ring around the central cylinder serve in the distribution of facilities to apartments, and are connected by arches to the pillars on the façade. This

74 ■ The organic form of the two towers contrasts with the pure and aseptic forms of International-Style skyscrapers. Their construction opened the way to many late-Modern buildings characterized by their original forms.

75 ■ The twin towers resembling corncobs stand beside the Chicago Canal in an area called "River North."

76 top ■ During the early phases of construction the structural system in which the floors were locked into the central column could be plainly seen. The aim was to allow the pillars in the façade to be lighter and slimmer.

76 center ■ When the model of the two towers was presented, it was clear that the goal was to break with the Modernist tradition popular at the time.

76 bottom ■ The plan shows the central structural core containing the facilities and the layout of the apartments with semi-circular balconies that face outward.

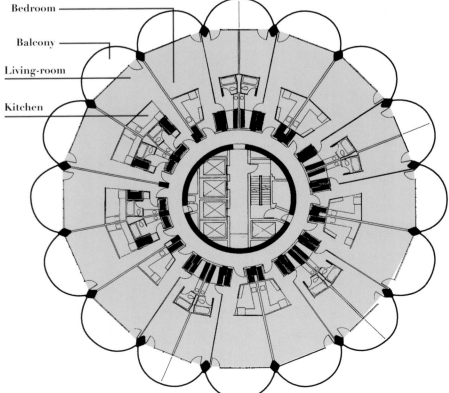

Bedroom

Balcony

Living-room

Kitchen

76-77 ■ The building during construction: the load-bearing structure and huge central column can be clearly seen.

78-79 ■ The unmistakable twin towers have been compared to enormous concrete flowers. The first 19 floors contain parking for 896 cars.

arrangement allows the structural elements of the façade, which must only support the vertical load, to be less bulky, thus also allowing for a significant reduction in materials. The towers were deliberately designed to resemble corncobs as a contrast to the pure and aseptic designs of contemporary skyscrapers. The semi-circular balconies that mark the end of the petal-shaped apartments ensure that the maximum amount of light enters the building. Although the structural system is apparent on the exterior, the towers were very innovative and in 1965 were awarded a prize by the New York Chapter of the American Institute of Architects.

Location	Project	Height	Materials	Completion date
Chicago (U.S.A.)	Bertrand Goldberg Associates	587 ft.	Steel, concrete, and glass	1962

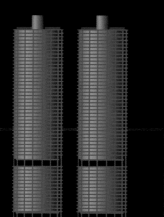

Lake Point Tower

The highly original Lake Point Tower appears like a prism extruding from a trilobate plan. Lined with a curtain-wall of reflecting glass, it dominates Lake Michigan from where it can be seen in its entirety from many different angles.

Its form resembles a design made for a skyscraper in 1922 by Mies van der Rohe (the architect of the Seagram Building) of whom the architects of Lake Point Tower were students. Whereas van der Rohe's design was based on a naturalistic form with a variable polylobate curve, Schipporeit-Heinrich's creation centers on a geometrical figure. The original design for this building bore greater similarity to van der Rohe's as it was based on a cross-shaped plan with four rounded arms, but these were later reduced to two to eliminate the problem of apartments facing each other directly. Finally, three arms set at an angle of 120 degrees were settled on to ensure each resident's privacy.

The external façade, a curtain-wall of reflecting glass chosen purposely to increase privacy, includes elements inserted between the floors to freshen the internal air supply, which also emphasize the horizontal aspect of the building. The result is that the aesthetic of the skyscraper is typical of International Style, though its eccentric form links it to late-Modernist towers like the Marina Towers (1962) with a

80 ▪ When it was completed in 1968, Lake Point Tower was the tallest apartment building in the world. An advantage of its particular structure is that it exposes a smaller surface area to the wind than more conventional rectangular-shaped buildings.

81 ▪ The trilobate building stands above a park that provides common space for the residents and acts as a link between the lake and the city.

LOCATION	PROJECT	HEIGHT	MATERIALS	COMPLETION DATE
CHICAGO (U.S.A.)	SCHIPPOREIT-HEINRICH ASSOCIATES WITH GRAHAM, ANDERSON, PROBST, AND WHITE	646 FT.	REINFORCED CONCRETE AND GLASS	1968

flower-shaped plan, the John Hancock Center (1969) with its truncated pyramid shape terminating in two large antennas, and the Transamerica Pyramid (1972), also in the shape of a pyramid. Another evident characteristic of the Lake Point Tower is its multifunctionality. This architectural theme, of which the Marina Towers are an example, was much emphasized in the 1960s and had its origin in the ideas of the Modernists. They believed that it was possible to design a complete, self-sufficient, and autonomous building in which inhabitants could find anything they required.

In tribute to this aspiration, Lake Point accommodates a number of recreational facilities in its lower floors and roof and has a park for the benefit of the residents that attempts to mediate between nature, as represented by the lake, and artifice, as represented by the urban environment. The body of the tower encompasses offices and 900 apartments. The reinforced concrete structure has a triangular core that contains the elevators and stairwell and absorbs horizontal forces. Thanks to this static system, the perimeter pillars on the façade can be less massive as they only have to bear vertical loads.

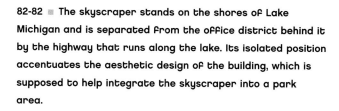

82-82 ■ The skyscraper stands on the shores of Lake Michigan and is separated from the office district behind it by the highway that runs along the lake. Its isolated position accentuates the aesthetic design of the building, which is supposed to help integrate the skyscraper into a park area.

83 top ■ From some angles it is possible to see the building as an isolated "object," surrounded only by the trees of the park and the boats on the lake.

83 bottom ■ Lake Point Tower is an original building in the midst of the towering skyline of the Loop in downtown Chicago. It stands on the lakefront like the vanguard of the skyscrapers in the business district.

John Hancock Center

Affectionately known as "Big John" for its size, the John Hancock Center was at the time of its construction one of the tallest skyscrapers in the world. Even today, it is still the most multifunctional, having commercial premises on the ground floor, a parking lot, offices from the 20th to 41st floors, and 711 apartments on the upper floors complete with services such as a post office and a supermarket. Right at the top there is an observation deck, a restaurant, and a bar that afford a superb view over the whole city. The services provided are so complete that residents and workers can satisfy all their needs within the building. This skyscraper is immediately recognizable in the Chicago skyline, in spite of the wide range of unusual and varying shapes in the city, thanks to its truncated-pyramid form (probably linked to the image of oil derricks) with antennas and the cross-shaped strengtheners to counter the force of the wind. The tendency to adopt strange forms instead of the traditional International-Style glass box — after precedents like Marina City Towers in Chicago — began in the 1970s when formal experimentation in buildings like San Francico's Transamerica Pyramid encouraged

84 ■ Like many giant buildings, the John Hancock Center in Chicago stands alone among the surrounding buildings, like an element unto itself. It is so tall that its residents truly live in a world apart: often they are not even aware of weather conditions on the ground.

85 ■ The great innovation of this skyscraper lies in its tubular structure resembling a large reticular beam, which allowed for a notable savings in steel with respect to traditional construction methods.

86-87 ■ The truncated pyramid shape, antennas, and cross-shaped strengtheners make "Big John" immediately recognizable on the Chicago skyline.

87 top ■ The tower is located on Michigan Avenue in one of the most attractive commercial areas of the city.

87 center ■ The decision to placing the structure in the façade creates greater opacity in terms of external appearance and the internal-external relationship.

87 bottom ■ Thanks to technical progress in various sectors, Fazlur Khan managed to create a structure able to effectively absorb both lateral forces caused by the wind and downward forces caused by gravity.

architects to incorporate a sculptural quality typical of late-Modernism in their designs. Big John stands on Michigan Avenue near the Lake Shore Drive Apartments designed by Mies van der Rohe. This is one of the most attractive commercial areas of the city, which is why the ground floor of the Hancock Center has a public space for commercial activities. It can be reached from the parking lot, which was largely overhauled in 1995 to include better lighting, a waterfall to hide the noise of the street, and new walkways for pedestrians. The innovation of this skyscraper was its tubular structure, like a large reticular beam. It was designed by Fazlur Khan (Sears Tower), who had a strong influence on the design of large buildings in the 1960s. During those years, great innovations in the field of structural design were made, thanks to the use of new software and improvements in steel quality. Such changes allowed Khan to design buildings with dimensions greater than those built previously. The structure is based on the placement of the various elements along the perimeter of the building with horizontal, vertical, and diagonal connections in order to form a very rigid steel tube able to counter the force of the wind. The consequences of this choice are an increase in load-bearing elements on the façade that cause greater opacity (both

JOHN HANCOCK CENTER

in terms of external appearance and internal-external relationship) and a different formulation of the integration of the public spaces on the lower floors. However, there is also a reduction in the thickness of the floors and a consequent reduction of the entire interfloor structure. Another corollary of placing structural elements in the facade is that the internal space remains open and can be organized with a greater degree of flexibility. The truncated pyramid form adapts well to the wealth of functionality offered, allowing the larger spaces on the lower floors to offer functions like parking and shops, whereas higher up, as the building tapers, the more restricted spaces are suited to residential accommodation. The façade, identifiable by the choice to make the structure of the building visible, is divided into five sections

Location	Project	Height	Materials	Completion date
Chicago (U.S.A.)	Bruce Graham of Skidmore, Owings, & Merrill	1,129 ft.	Steel, aluminum, and glass	1969

each of 18 floors designated by diagonal tubes, with an additional half section of nine floors at the top. The façade is lined with anodized aluminum and bronze-colored glass. On the very top of the building, two 330-foot antennas (radio and television) give the building an even more imposing appearance. Visible from a great distance, when they are lit up at night they become a distinctive feature of the Chicago skyline.

88-89 ■ An observation deck, a restaurant, and a bar at the top of the skyscraper afford splendid views over all of Chicago and Lake Michigan. However, what really makes the building unmistakable are its two huge radio and television antennas.

Pyramid

90 and 91 ■ The façade of the Transamerica Pyramid is characterized by alternating filled horizontal bands, lined with panels made of a special hardened quartz-aggregate paste, and rows of windows.

Transamerica Pyramid

Commissioned to design the headquarters of one of America's most important financial companies, the Transamerica Corporation, American architect William Pereira justified his choice of a pyramid shape with three reasons: it allowed him to evade regulations that govern the height of a building relative to the ground area it occupies, it provides greater light and air at street level, and transforms the tower into an advertisement of the Transamerica Corporation's power. It differed from all the other skyscrapers built in International Style in the United States until that time, which take the form of a pure crystal prism, and presented itself as an icon, a symbol, and the promoter of a message. This modification in architectural language during the early 1970s came at a moment of great change both in architecture (the great masters like Wright, Le Corbusier, van der Rohe, and Gropius had all died between 1959-69 and the Modernists' idea that a building was determined by its function started to lose importance) and in social and political fields, as interest in themes such as ecology and respect

Location	Project	Height	Materials	Completion date
San Francisco (U.S.A.)	William L. Pereira & Associates	853 ft.	Steel, reinforced cement, and quartz aggregate	1972

93 top ▪ The tower stands in the center of San Francisco, one of the cities in America most protective of its history and characterized by numerous Beaux-Arts-style buildings.

92-93 ▪ The skyscraper has a strong impact on the San Francisco panorama with its steep hills and roads, Eclectic-style architecture, and bridges over the bay.

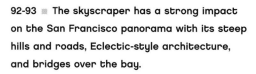

92 bottom ▪ The pyramidal shape of the tower contrasts sharply with its surroundings. In the wake of the architectural experimentation of the time, the building has become a sort of sculpture of strong symbolic value.

for the environment became more popular. Information was more freely available, lifestyles became looser, and futuristic cities were imagined. In this cultural panorama, architecture too was freed from the dogmas of the past and new formal experiments attempted to incorporate other artistic disciplines, in particular, sculpture. The Transamerica Pyramid grew out of this background of late-Modern architectural formalism, however, it was not accepted favorably by the public, who found it cumbersome and out of context. With a wealth of Beaux-Arts buildings, San Francisco is one of the cities in America that prides itself most on its history and, more than any other, has strict regulations to control planning and construction of new buildings. The city's first urban development plan of 1839 was based on a orthogonal grid that was superimposed over the orography of the area without much consideration. One of San Francisco's fundamental characteristics is its landscape, with steep, hilly roads, Eclectic-style architecture, and bridges criss-crossing its bay. Today, the Transamerica Pyramid, which stands in the business district between Montgomery Street and Columbus Avenue, is visible from every point in the city and has become one of the city's symbols. Being in an earth-

TRANSAMERICA PYRAMID

Transamerica
PYRAMID

quake-prone zone, the tower was designed with anti-seismic techniques: between the second and fifth floors, its base is formed by twenty connected isosceles tetrahedrons joined to the foundations by steel girders that create a rigid spatial truss. Above the tetrahedrons and visible from the exterior, its façade is characterized by filled horizontal bands made from a special hardened quartz-based paste and rows of windows. The very top of the building, where the space is too small for offices (only a small observation deck for the public exists on the 27th floor), has continuous facing, as do the two wings of the pyramid that contain the elevators and emergency stairs. The location of the elevators and stairs is due more to a logistical formality than an economical solution, in the sense that the elevators should require less and less space as the building rises. Despite the many and vociferous protests the tower aroused during its construction, with the passing of time it has become a symbol of the city and is now accepted and recognized as a reference point by most of the residents of San Francisco.

Montparnasse Tower

Soaring with a minimal curtain wall, isolated in the verticality that conflicts with the horizontality of the ordinary, average-height city buildings heavily decorated with pilasters, balconies, and attics that surround it, the Tour Montparnasse stands like a monolith over the commercial buildings below. It seems to come from another world, that of a more mature modern and International Style, and creates such a contrast that it forces one to stop and stare. It was built to be the largest office block in Europe.

Its appearance as an object of industrial design fallen from heaven – or at least uprooted from the history of urban landscape – is emphasized by its strange geometry, resembling the Pirelli building in Milan or the Pan Am building in New York, and which is coherent with the stylistic trends of the 1950s. The slightly convex 197-foot-long sides of the skyscraper's long, thin shape and its single volume with profiled sheath, utterly differentiate the tower from the regularity of the buildings in the adjacent blocks, on which the normative for the central area of the city imposes a height of roughly 85 feet. The dimensions, character, and location of this tower constitute significant contributions to the contrast between the skyscraper – an innovative architectural typology essentially linked to the general grid-like conception of American cities –

96 ■ Montparnasse Tower seems an object of industrial design fallen from heaven, completely unrelated to the history of the Parisian urban landscape.

97 ■ Characterized by the use of a curtain wall, which has repetitive forms typical of the most classic American skyscrapers, the tower contrasts with the horizontality and decorations of the ordinary city buildings surrounding it.

MONTPARNASSE TOWER

and the European city based on typological and morphological rules laid down over time. The privilege of verticality over the general city spread is generally only conferred on large monuments of religious or political significance, in recognition of their function as an element of public order. This attribute is clearly demonstrated in Victor Hugo's fascinating description of Paris seen from important points, most notably of which the bell-towers of Notre Dame. The world capital of the nineteenth century, Paris is the city where the Eiffel Tower stands. The tower was the world's tallest structure until the construction of the Chrysler Building and was the subject of a fierce debate between those who wanted it to remain standing after the international exhibition, for which it was built as a positive symbol of modernity, and those who wished it to be taken down as it represented overly violent imposition of modernity on the traditional and historical inheritance of the city. The debate was even more intense over the Montparnasse Tower, mostly because the tall building represented the culmination of an operation of urban re-

newal (the reuse of the old railway station) that threatened to overwhelm the longstanding fabric of a district that symbolized historical, cultural, intellectual, and artistic Paris and replace it with a series of infrastructural and multifunctional hubs intended for commercial activities and offices. Moreover, this urban renewal program was scheduled to last until 1934. The use of tall buildings in Paris, in the style of American skyscrapers, was restricted to external districts, even though La Défense attempted to create a thread of continuity between the historical layout of the city through its axis that runs from the Louvre through the Arc du Carousel and from the Arc de Triomphe along the Champs Elysées. With several other buildings of the period, for instance in Genoa and Milan, the Montparnasse Tower was the prototype of projects to locate multifunctional high-rise buildings in city centers, with the purpose of increasing the economic and symbolic value of obsolete districts. This approach has since been copied in London, Vienna, Rotterdam, and Madrid. Montparnasse Tower is now a focal point of the Parisian skyline.

Location	Project	Height	Materials	Completion date
Paris (France)	Baudoin, Cassan, de Marien, and Saubot	689 ft.	Steel and glass	1973

Sears Tower

The tallest building in Chicago is currently the tallest in the northern hemisphere and worldwide is topped only by the Petronas Towers in Kuala Lumpur. The Sears Tower, however, holds the record for having the highest occupied floor, as the Petronas Towers are only higher thanks to their antennas.

The Sears Tower, fully completed in 1974, was conceived within the context of "the height war," fought mostly between New York and Chicago (it was never considered that the record might actually pass to an Asian city, though Skidmore, Owings, & Merrill eventually worked there as well). It was built as a kind of revenge against the Twin Towers, to confirm once more the predominance of the city of production over the city of finance. The Sears Tower is a fundamental feature of the Chicago skyline. After being the first city to have high-rise buildings in the central Loop district, the zones surrounding downtown began to sprout towers of original designs, including the twin cylinders of Marina City, the truncated pyramid of the John Hancock building, the Aon Center, and Lake Point with its unusual volumes. The result is a panorama of extraordinary structures over which the Sears building dominates (it is 312 feet higher than the John Hancock and 305 feet taller than the Aon Center), making it a visual and symbolic landmark for the whole city.

100 ■ Two huge antennas rise from the roof of Chicago's tallest skyscraper, rising over 1,450 feet from the ground. Buildings in the surrounding forest of skyscrapers seem small compared to the Sears Tower.

101 ■ The Sears Tower rises high over Chicago, whose skyline is filled with towers of unusual designs. Obviously the dominant feature, it is a symbol and visual reference point for the whole city.

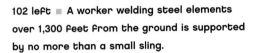

102 left ■ A worker welding steel elements over 1,300 feet from the ground is supported by no more than a small sling.

102 right ■ On May 3, 1973, the flags of Chicago and the United States were raised at the top of the Sears Tower to celebrate the "topping out".

On clear days, visibility can reach up to 40-50 miles from the sky deck, meaning that four states can be seen: Illinois, Indiana, Wisconsin, and Michigan.

It was built for the consumer goods corporation of Sears, Roebuck, and Company, which wished to unite its 10,000 employees and 6,000, tenants together under one roof.

The twin requirements of building high and having as much natural light in the open-space offices as possible led to an innovative structural principle and to a highly recognizable distribution of volumes. Nine megastructural tubes stand as though in a sheaf on the base, flexing inwards as they rise, but only two of which reach the top of the building. Together they create a very modern version of an asymmetrical ziggurat.

The structure based on the group of autonomous tubes (each structural module measures 75 and a half feet on each side and the columns stand at an interval of 15 feet) seems ideal for the mutual collaboration of the struc-

tures in absorbing both the vertical loads and the horizontal forces created by the wind. The square base rises to the 50th floor. Seven tubes rise symmetrically on one diagonal to the 66th floor, five symmetrically in a cross design to the 90th, and just two laterally in a rectangular plan up to the 108th floor. Above this level emerge the two antennas.

The horizontal bands of the service floors every 328 feet, which are characterized by a differently designed façade, mark the distribution of volumes. The elevator equipment is housed on the service floors. Only some of the elevators serve the entire building from the basement as far as the crowning terrace; others give access to particular service floors where it is possible to switch to other elevators (always in a different position) that serve the next set of floors. The four topmost floors below the upper deck contain four ventilation systems.

The architects of this building also designed the John Hancock Building – better known as "Big John" – and in fact both buildings boast a "vision-

103 ■ This view from a helicopter taken during the tower's crowning ceremony shows, both the relationship between the Sears Tower and the surrounding buildings and the internal structure of the skyscraper, still lacking its façade.

Location	Project	Height	Materials	Completion date
Chicago (U.S.A.)	Bruce Graham of Skidmore, Owings, & Merrill	1450 ft.	Steel, aluminum, and glass	1974

104 ■ The skyscraper resembles a modern asymmetrical ziggurat.

105 top left ■ Ten thousand workers fill the building each day. Here we see the atrium.

ary" constructional innovation coherently articulated in strongly visual figures that form the plastic expression of the static, technological, and distributive system. To Louis Sullivan, the tapering of a skyscraper toward the top was its principal aspect, and here it is performed by the articulation of the structure that functions like a large "shelf" attached to the ground and resistant to the force of the wind. This resistance is created by the arrangement of the tubular structures (operating as "wall-based" resisters) into sets of four vertical pillars. The process of progressive contraction of the volumes is governed by the geometry of the axis of the center of gravity and its axes of frontal and diagonal symmetry.

The Sears Tower is one of Skidmore, Owings, & Merrill's most important creations. SOM is a extremely organized architectural group that can work at the highest levels, using the most advanced technology. It is able to produce widely varying designs for sites around the world that meet the very different requirements of its clients and markets. In 1952, SOM designed Lever House in New York, which has been described as the "progenitor of the American-style skyscraper." It was given a curtain-wall "box" shape that was later copied widely and applied by SOM in Chicago to the Civic Center in 1965. After the John Hancock and Sears Towers, SOM produced the Jin Mao, or "pagoda of technology," in Shanghai in 1998.

105 top right and bottom ■ On the ground floor, strongly modeled flights of steps cross the atrium illuminated by enormous windows. Today, the entrance welcomes over 25,000 people per day.

106-107 ■ Chicago's amazing skyline can be admired from the Skydeck at the top of the building.

Peachtree Plaza Hotel

At 725 feet, the Peachtree Plaza is the tallest hotel in the United States. Its cylindrical tower, which is lit up at night, stands out in the Atlanta panorama, even though today it is no longer isolated as it was when completed in 1976. Its presence contributes to giving Atlanta the appearance of an international city visited by people from all over the world.

Its architect and promoter, John Portman, was astute enough to recognize that architecture can be used to communicate a promotional message and, at the same time, be viewed as goods on display, a concept defined by historian Manfredo Tafuri as "the commercialization of typologies." In a country and during a period ruled by free trade, Portman became the symbol of consumerism in the field of architecture. His designs were meant to exceed limits, making use of highly apparent, self-promoting elements, as if architecture, like all goods, could and had to be advertised and sold.

108 and 109 ■ The 725 feet of the purely cylindrical Peachtree Plaza Hotel stand out against the Atlanta skyline. The hotel is made even more immaterial by the use of reflecting glass everywhere except for the revolving restaurant at the top, from where the panorama of the whole city can be enjoyed.

110 top and 111 ■ John Portman designs hotels with spectacular and dazzling interiors. These buildings are first and foremost commercial constructions that have to provide a certain profitability and be self-promoting. The combination of clever techniques and cheap materials provides the basis for this aspect of Portman's designs.

Portman produced many hotels in the United States, all in a similar late-Modern style, featuring spectacular and dazzling spaces belonging to fantasy worlds. Yet at the same time, being a good promoter of his architecture, he ensured that his designs were feasible and profitable to their owners. The size of a hotel is dictated by its economic returns, and reinforced concrete is the building material of choice precisely because it is the cheapest available and the quickest to build with. The Peachtree Plaza Hotel is made entirely from reinforced concrete. It has a central core that supports the loads of the entire tower and contains the elevators and stairways. The base of the building discharges the loads through huge pylons and trusses (also made

Location	Project	Height	Materials	Completion date
ATLANTA (U.S.A.)	JOHN PORTMAN & ASSOCIATES	725 FT.	REINFORCED CONCRETE AND GLASS	1976

110 bottom ■ Inside, the base of the skyscraper contains meeting rooms, bars, shops, and other public spaces. There is a large atrium resembling a covered piazza that is characterized by volumes of different heights. Internal terraces of different heights, covered by glass and steel surfaces, face onto one another.

from concrete) placed around the perimeter of the building. The concrete base that covers the entire lot contrasts with the crystalline image given by the height of the skyscraper and the smaller tower that encloses the elevators. Portman's philosophy is that a hotel should also be a part of the city within the city, in which the guest-consumer can find all the services he requires to satisfy his needs. The base contains conference rooms, bars, shops, and other public spaces, while the top of the tower boasts a revolving restaurant that looks out over the entire city.

112-113 and 113 right ■ Lined with a continuous curtain-wall of reflecting glass, the curved façade of the hotel reflects neighboring buildings and the light in ever different ways.

112 bottom ■ The atrium is deliberately monumental, with overlooking terraces and escalators that create a space in which the various activities of the hotel take place so as to seem like an ever-changing stage. The presence of water in this common area is part of both an attempt to maintain a link between man and nature and a love for games and fantasy that recurs throughout all of Portland's buildings.

114 and 115 ■ With its cylindrical tower, the Peachtree Plaza Hotel lights up at night like a crystal. Its designer used glass in order to create a sense of unity with nature and the space that, beyond the curtain wall, surrounds the guests in their rooms.

The atrium alone constitutes a microcosm of the city. It is built on various levels with internal terraces and escalators that face one another and which together create a monumental space that allow the observer to watch everything that is going on within the hotel. The atrium also contains a 18-inche-deep pool of water with waterfalls, suspended terraces, plants, birds, and fish recalling the Hanging Gardens of Babylon and the Tivoli Gardens in Copenhagen. The effect of Portman's designs on the users of his buildings is what brings his hotels so much success.

Citicorp Center

Citicorp Center

Despite being situated in the dense urban fabric of Manhattan, the Citicorp Center is one of the skyscrapers that succeed in standing out in the New York skyline thanks to its 45-degree sloping roof, and owing to the extraordinary and innovative space it has made available to the public by being raised entirely off the ground. This aspect has created a practice that serves as an example to be followed by many others. As its architect Hugh Stubbins explained in a letter written in 1970 to his client, Henry J. Muller (then Vice-President of the First National Bank), his intent was "to use the means of large companies, rich in moral and social ideas, to create a new series of office buildings designed for one and all, to be an expression of the individuals who use them." The possibility to create this public space was due partly to the advanced ideas of the designer and partly to the fact that the Lutheran church of St. Peter had occupied 30 percent of the site on which it was built since 1862. An agreement was reached stipulating that the church would be demolished following sale of the site but that a new chapel would be built on the same land. Thus, the body of the building was raised 100 feet from the ground by four enormous pylons positioned in the center of each side so as allow the creation of a public space uninterrupted by pylons too closely

116 ■ The roof of the skyscraper is angled at 45 degrees, which differentiates it from the many other skyscrapers in Manhattan.

117 bottom ■ Raised off the ground on four enormous pylons, Citicorp Center features an open public space at its base that has the double effect of livening up an otherwise square and regular structure and giving new life to an area that, had it been reserved exclusively for offices, may have been impersonal.

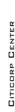

positioned to one another. Several structures were built in this area, among them the new St. Peter's Church, the entrance to the subway station, and a large space in the form of an amphitheater. The space helped to ensure the popularity of the building and also gave useful hints for the drawing-up of new regulations on public spaces in order to lessen the density of constructions in Manhattan at ground level. Because Citicorp Center was built during a period of economic recession following the first oil crisis, the building made use of many structural and technical innovations. The weight of the building was carried by the core and four pylons (which contain the elevators and stairs), above which a steel structure divides the building into six sections of eight stories, each composed of vertical pillars corresponding to a pylon and V-shaped horizontal and diagonal trusses to counter the effect of the wind. Other innovations were energy saving systems like the heat recovery system, energy-saving illumination, and two-level elevators. Another idea was the addition of a dampener formed by a 440-ton block of concrete to soften oscillations caused by the wind. Placed on the roof and connected to a computer, it moves in order to reduce fluctuations caused by wind forces by 50 percent. The façade has thin horizontal bands alternating with shiny aluminum panels and reflecting glass to give the building a vibrant image that immediately distinguishes it from the wealth of skyscrapers found in this area of New York.

Location	Project	Height	Materials	Completion date
New York (U.S.A.)	Hugh Stubbins & Associates with Emery Roth & Sons	915 ft.	Steel, aluminum, and glass	1977

118-119 ■ The idea to create a public space with various services at the base of the Citicorp Center originated partly from a need to provide some breathing space in a high-density area where buildings rise next to one another like trees in a forest.

119 top right ■ Though situated in an area of the city densely populated by other skyscrapers, Citicorp Center stands out for its original design and shiny cladding.

119 bottom ■ The hollow internal space onto which the building's floors face contributes to the originality of the skyscraper's design and its greater habitability compared to traditional New York prisms.

National Commercial Bank

This building features a triangular prism entirely closed on the outside with the exception of three large windows that break the continuity of two of the three façades. The third façade is characterized by a parallelepiped that contains the elevators and stairs and, at the top, by a strip of small windows that create a sort of minimalist frame. It has an unusual appearance and is original in that it does not attempt – unlike other skyscrapers in Arab countries – to create a bizarre, symbolic form. Instead, its pure volume stands out isolated in the desert panorama. Jeddah developed enormously following the spread of Islam in the sixth century, being a port city and a stopping point for pilgrims on their way to the holy city of Mecca. Recently, it has grown as a financial center and, thanks to its port on the Red Sea, as a commercial center that trades mostly with the West.

120 ■ The National Commercial Bank, on the shore of the Red Sea, is a clean smooth surfaced prism. It seems to attract light and heat in great quantities; it actually deals with local climatic demands perfectly.

121 bottom ■ The entrance is marked by a cantilever roof supported by cross-shaped pillars, both lined with granite like the rest.

122 ■ The cylindrical volume of the concrete 400-space parking lot rests against the prism. *Chiaroscuro* geometrical motifs can be seen on the base.

Location	Project	Height	Materials	Completion date
Jeddah (Saudi Arabia)	Skidmore, Owings, & Merrill	400 ft.	Steel, concrete, and travertine	1983

123 top left ■ The drawing shows a cross-section of the building. As the external walls are closed, all the offices face onto triangular inner courtyards that interrupt the uniform surface of the façades with three large apertures 105 feet wide.

123 top right ■ The garden on the roof of the base can be glimpsed through the hollow triangular space that runs down the center of the building.

123 bottom ■ The general plan shows the isolation of the group of buildings in an area surrounded by fast, busy highways. It also shows how the triangular parallelepiped of the skyscraper and the circular volume of the parking lot both rise out of the base covering the entire lot.

The clients of this building wished to build the headquarters of the National Commercial Bank here and so commissioned Skidmore, Owings & Merrill, who had designed the Hajj Terminal in Jeddah in 1982, to oversee the project to build a highly technological tower covered with glass-fiber where pilgrims traveling to Mecca could rest. The National Commercial Bank building was designed as a triangular tower of 27 stories flanked by a round concrete parking lot for 400 automobiles. Although the architects based their design on western skyscrapers, they reinterpreted it in an Islamic fashion, lining the outer walls of the tower with travertine to create an appearance of mass and volume. This contrasts with the western approach in which the goal is to endow the building with lightness and to reduce its material impact. The fact that the building faces inward and that the windows on the external walls are blind is derived from the principles of Islamic tradition but also has a functional motive: to protect the building's residents from the heat and excessive sunlight. All the offices face onto internal triangular courtyards that cut the façades with three large apertures each measuring 105 feet wide. Two of them, each seven floors high, are on the south side and look toward the old

124-125 ■ The National Commercial Bank offers, a panoramic view of Jeddah, generally characterized by rather low buildings.

125 top right ■ The plans show a triangle-shaped cross-section of the tower's office space. Thanks to its geometric purity, the skyscraper has been defined one of the most abstract creations of its type ever built.

125 center and bottom ■ The decoration of the hall, as well as the other interiors, is based on a recurrent triangle motif and is composed of marble and other high-quality materials from all over the world.

city; the other, nine floors high, sits on the northeast side and faces out to sea. Thus, the National Commercial Bank is a naturally ecological building. By eliminating the external windows, the costs of heating and air-conditioning are lowered, because the three staggered courtyards and empty center create a sort of natural flue that draws the heat up out of the building. The light inside the building is therefore never direct but is filtered through the three large apertures. The structure was built in reinforced concrete further strengthened at the corners while the elevators, stairways, and facilities were placed in a separate section. Although elevator and stair systems are usually used to provide the structure with rigidity, this was an innovative choice for the towers. In this building, the structure is continuous and placed along the edge of the plan, allowing the triangular hall to remain completely free. Both the hall and the offices are decorated with marble and other precious materials from around the world.

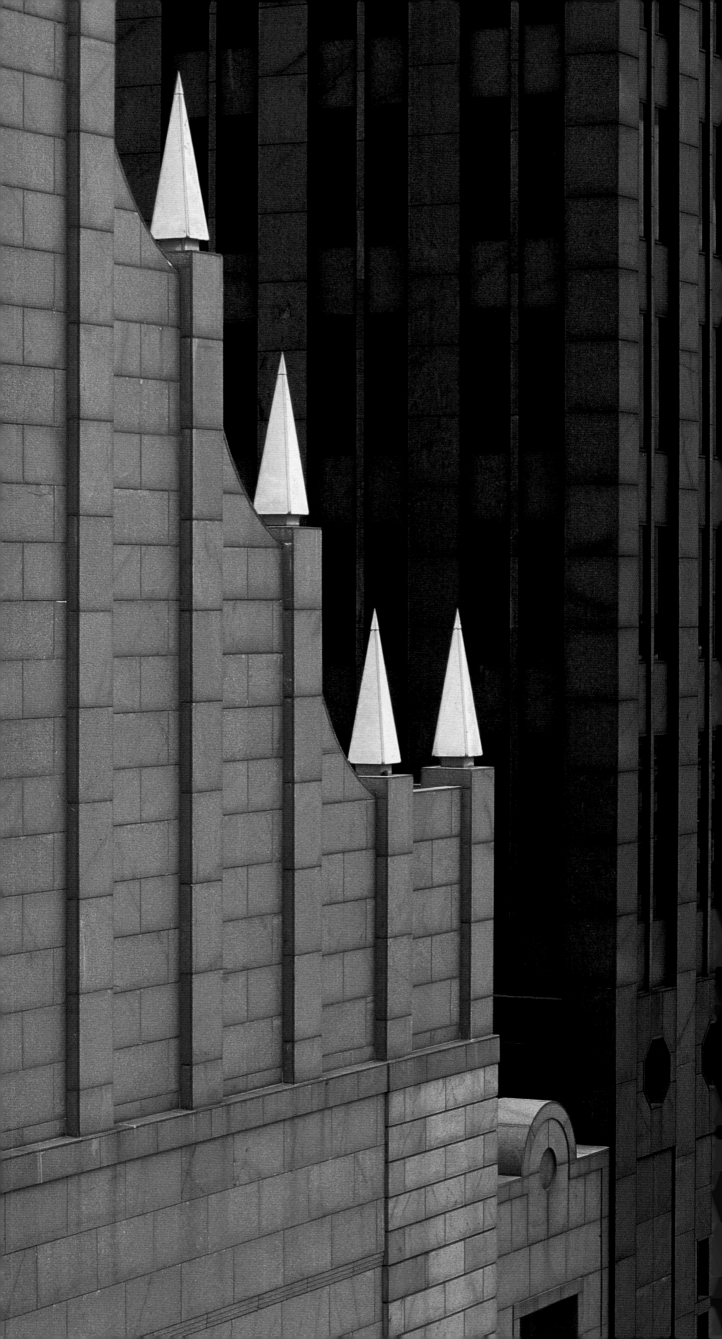

NationsBank Center

NationsBank Center

The NationsBank Center of Houston, previously known as the Republic Bank Center, consists of two buildings in downtown Houston and is a monumental work by Philip Johnson, the great American architect and champion of the International Style. He designed many skyscrapers, including the Seagram Building with Mies van der Rohe in 1958. The NationsBank project was completed in 1984 during a period in which the architect had abandoned International Style and found inspiration in historical eclecticism. He had already used this tactic in his design of the AT&T building (in New York) of the same year, which was his first office skyscraper. Johnson discarded the glass-box approach and instead used traditional materials like granite, searching for various styles in architectural history that could be assimilated eclectically into his design.

NationsBank Center occupies an entire lot in Houston's commercial district. The city was founded in 1836 on marshy, unhealthy terrain and laid out on a grid that runs northeast to southwest. During the years following its foundation, and even recently, the city has undergone an extraordinary but haphazard development process due to having no urban plan,

126 ■ The façade of this building was designed in an eclectic style that makes use of motifs and elements from architectural history, such as pinnacles rising from the gables of the tower similar to those of the Gothic cathedrals of Northern Europe. The idea was to give the building a strong identity in Houston, an urban setting without much history.

127 ■ The NationsBank Center stands in downtown Houston. It is made recognizable by the three setbacks lined by thin, tall gables on its façade that help to it to blend harmoniously with the surrounding buildings.

128 top ■ NationsBank Center comprises two buildings: the lower one, on the left, in which take place public functions, and the 56-story tower that contains offices.

128 bottom ■ Like its exterior, the interior of the NationsBank Center is characterized by post-modern elements like the two series of arches that enclose the space occupied by a pedestal clock.

129 ■ The low building has a large hall covered by a series of vaults. These allow the light to filter unevenly from above to create a special atmosphere.

LOCATION	PROJECT	HEIGHT	MATERIALS	COMPLETION DATE
HOUSTON (U.S.A.)	JOHNSON/BURGEE ARCHITECTS	781 FT.	STEEL AND GRANITE	1983

but it can nonetheless boast many brilliant examples of contemporary architecture. The city consists of many different neighborhoods, of which downtown is the most important. It is composed almost entirely of offices and skyscrapers, including the NationsBank, which, despite its 781 feet, does not stand out as part of the city skyline. The first of the two buildings is a small, 12-story volume containing a pre-existing building that could not be demolished and a large functional hall open to the public. The second one is a 56-story tower that contains the offices. The base of the tower is the same height as the lower building and so creates a link between the two. The tower is conventional in that its façade is divided into a stone-faced base, an intermediate section, and a crown. The crown has three stepbacks that create a scalar relationship with the surrounding buildings, and each stagger is covered by a tall, tight gable resembling those of northern European houses, particularly in Holland. The spacing of the light aluminum ribs that produce a *chiaroscuro* effect and confer a sculptural quality on the building emphasizes the vertical aspect of the façade. The structure is composed of a steel skeleton. The low building has a reinforced concrete structure lined with granite and a roof formed by a network of vaults that let in light from above, thus creating a space that brings to mind those of the Ancient Romans.

Hong Kong and Shanghai Bank

The Hong Kong skyline is strongly characterized by eccentric designs like Norman Foster's Hong Kong and Shanghai Bank and Pei's Bank of China. These two famous international architects stress the use of advanced technologies in their designs so that their buildings are immediately recognizable and visible, rising to the level – in this case – of symbols of the worldwide economic power of this ex-British colony. Located in the heart of the financial district, the headquarters of the Hong Kong and Shanghai Bank occupies a 587-foot-high building that is also one of the world's most technologically advanced structures, and, having cost $600 million, is also one of the most costly. It stands in one of the most central and attractive parts of the city, in line with the Star Ferry Terminal, from which it is separated by a large, open green area. The building stands next to the classical-style Courthouse, and the contrast between the brick mass of the Courthouse and the modern exterior of the

130 ■ The short sides of the building contain the vertical distribution equipment and facilities.

131 ■ The headquarters of the Hong Kong and Shanghai Bank is one of the world's most technologically advanced buildings. The contrast with the adjacent Classical-style Courthouse accentuates the structure's modern appearance.

Location	Project	Height	Materials	Completion date
Hong Kong (China)	Norman Foster & Partners	587 ft.	Steel, aluminum, and glass	1985

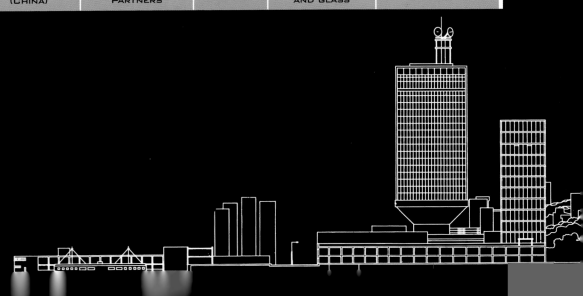

bank emphasizes the latter's use of advanced technology. When Foster won the competition in 1978, and even when the building was finally completed in 1986, Hong Kong was still under British rule and it was believed to remain so. Thus, the construction of this new office block was to represent not only one of the most important banks in East Asia, but also Hong Kong as a British colony in a far-away overseas territory. The structure of the building is completely innovative. It consists of two rows of four massive metal trellis pylons, formed by four pillars each, that stand along the shorter sides of the rectangular plan. They are spaced at intervals of 53 feet and connected to those parallel to them by a truss that covers a span of 110 feet, is two stories high, and that looks like a suspension bridge. The structure has five such trusses, one above another, to bear the loads created by the building above, and in this way the thickness of the floors and the various stories above could be reduced substantially. For each of these trusses, open spaces, terraces, and fireproof shelters divide the building vertically into five sections of different heights. The trusses that cross the building longitudinally form a sort of giant order that are completely "out of scale" compared to the placement of the windows, making

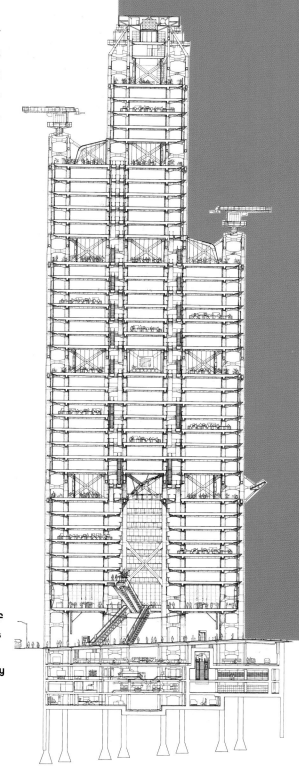

132 top ■ The glass elevators in the top portion of the building give riders a spectacular view.

132-133 bottom ■ The drawing (B) of the building's city location shows the bank next to the Courthouse and aligned with the Star Ferry Terminal. The building looks down toward the port over a park and out over the bay.

133 top ■ The transversal section (A) gives an idea of the building's structure composed of two rows of four massive pylons made of metal trellis along the short sides of the rectangle. They are spaced at regular intervals and connected to those parallel by a truss that functions like a suspension bridge. This complex system is obvious even from the outside of the building since the structure was purposely not given a curtain wall.

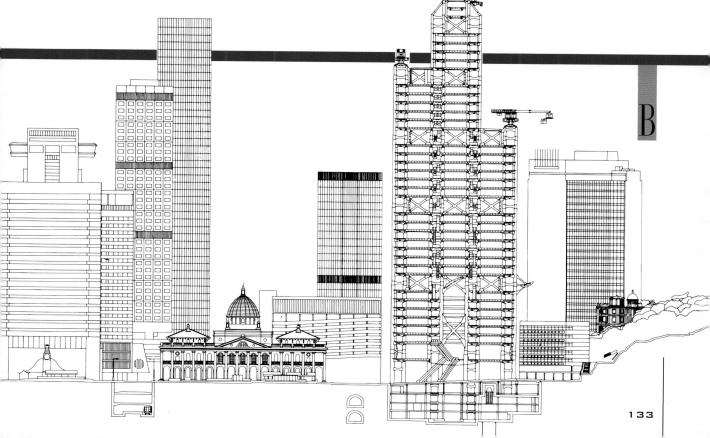

134 top ■ A curved glass roof provides a cover for the public area below, connected to the big atrium by an escalator.

134 bottom ■ The enormous hollow space containing the 52-story atrium gets light both from the transparent floor and the ceiling of reflective glass.

135 ■ Because the system of trusses leaves room for ample windows, activity within the offices can be seen in what seems like a monument to hard work and productivity. Similarly, activity in the street can be easily observed from the offices.

136-137 ■ The trusses across the building are the most characteristic elements of the two main façades, which are even more visible when lit up at night.

them a characteristic feature of the two main façades. The two other faces are distinguished by the elevator and facility elements. The placing of the structural elements and elevators on the façades (unlike traditional skyscrapers where they are housed in the structure's core) frees up the central space, thus allowing it to be used more flexibly in the organization of offices and other spaces. The most unusual feature of the entire building is the enormous 171-foot-high space in which the atrium is located. The atrium has a curved glass floor that forms the ceiling of a large open public space at street level and that is connected to the atrium by an escalator giving access to the building. There is also a mirrored ceiling in which computer-controlled panels can be adjusted to reflect the maximum quantity of natural light into the interior. Combined with the light entering through the glass ceiling, this large space is extraordinarily luminous, such that the ten floors of offices facing onto it draw much of their illumination from it. The façades, characterized by the intersection of the horizontal trusses and the vertical trellis pylons, are lined with gray aluminum and full-height, double-glazed panels.

Bank Tower

First Interstate Bank Tower

The First Interstate Bank Tower Complex – formerly known as the Allied Bank Tower – comprises twin towers resembling crystal prisms. They are perpendicular to one another and askew within the layout of the lot. They stand in an area situated on the outskirts of the central commercial district of Dallas, and for this reason its owners wanted the building to be a spectacular, awesome sight, able to attract leasers and buyers even though their location was not central.

The first tower of the complex houses bank offices; its twin, built two years later, contains a hotel. Between the two is a square that clearly demonstrates the influence of previously conceived public spaces such as those at the base of the Citicorp Center in New York and at Philip Johnson's Pennzoil Place in Houston. Unlike these earlier buildings, the First Interstate Bank features an open space with a geometric garden called "Fountain Place," designed by the landscape artist Daniel Kiley. The garden stands on an orthogonal grid that covers all the open area on the lot and boasts 217 fountains that alternate with cypress trees. The aim of the garden was to provide a tranquil spot where

138 ▣ The tower is clad with panels of reflecting glass mounted so that the joints are invisible. In consequence, the building seems different from every angle depending on the point of view and weather conditions, as if it were a geometric shape in perpetual movement.

139 ▣ The tower stands out as a dominant feature in the area. Underneath its pure and simple appearance, complex patterns and an extremely sophisticated steel support structure are hidden.

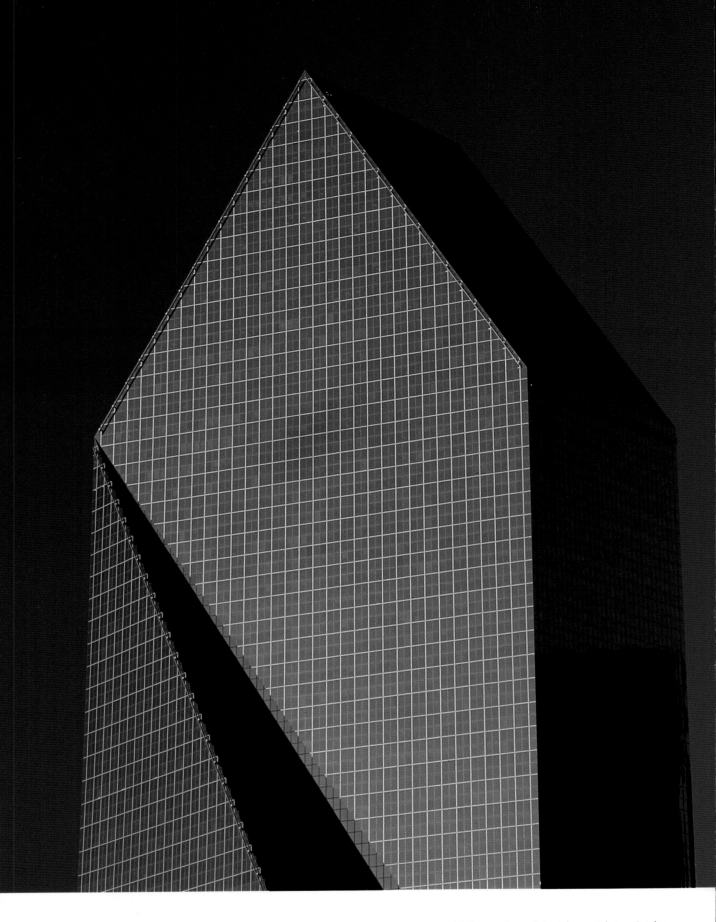

140-141 ■ Salient characteristics of the building are its reflective lining and its unusual shape ending in a triangular prism. The skyscraper stands on the edge of the business district in Dallas where the low, featureless buildings often display colorful murals to add a note of creativity.

nature could be enjoyed in the midst of the hurly-burly of highways, parking lots, and shops. Downtown Dallas has developed relatively recently on the model of downtown Manhattan, and features fast-moving streets and modern, box-shaped skyscrapers scattered rather haphazardly. With their sculptural form, the two towers are a defining element in the otherwise gray and monotonous, even though chaotic, downtown landscape. They rise up from a square base measuring 192 feet per side above which stands a ten-faced polygonal

LOCATION	PROJECT	HEIGHT	MATERIALS	COMPLETION DATE
DALLAS (U.S.A.)	HENRY COBB OF PEI, COBB, FREED	719 FT.	STEEL, ALUMINUM, AND GLASS	1985

volume composed of tetrahedrons and rhombuses, finally topped by a triangular prism. Corresponding to this geometrical system is a load-bearing structure formed by tubes similar to those used in the John Hancock Center in Chicago, but in this case they are hidden behind the façade. The system of tubes is composed of horizontal, vertical, and diagonal tubes and functions like a large reticular 40-story truss. This is formed, in turn, by eight smaller reticular systems that stand on top of one another. The gable is fashioned from a single Vierendeel truss supported by closely spaced pillars. The building is lined with plates of reflecting green glass, a material previously used by the architect of the John Hancock Tower in Boston in his effort to achieve the same effect of a pure prism free of material substance. The First Interstate Bank Tower was, at the time of its construction, the tallest building in the world among those lined with plates of silicon glass. Installed so that the joints are not visible, the plates give the building the appearance of an ever-changing minimalist sculpture that takes on a different appearance at any angle from which it is viewed. The same architects continued in the same vein when they designed the Bank of China Building in Hong Kong four years later. This splendid structure also has a complex distribution of volumes based on a basic triangular shape using materials with strong visual impact.

Lipstick Building

Lipstick Building

Situated on the corner of Third Avenue and 53rd Street, next to the Citicorp Center, this building is extraordinary for its original, elliptical form. Breaking away from the rigid orthogonal layout of Manhattan and neighboring buildings, all of which are regular parallelepipeds, has become one of New York's most famous buildings. Its architect, Philip Johnson, describes it as "an oval building in a rectangular setting." In addition to the elliptical form, on three levels the blocks retreat toward the top of the building to create an innovative distribution of volumes. When combined with the red granite facing, the building suggested the shape of that most famous of feminine accessories, lipstick, from whence comes its nickname. Even if Philip Johnson never believed in sculptural architecture, in the Lipstick Building he created a plastic object that adds a unique form to the New York skyline despite not being particularly high. It seems to evoke the pop sculptures of Claes Oldenburg representing everyday objects.

What Johnson has done is to create an analogy – unlike other designs of his featuring elements taken from history – with a commonly used object (a lipstick). This unusual

142 ■ For the façade of the Lipstick Building in New York, Philip Johnson chose to not apply post-modern motifs as he had in his other creations of the 1980s, such as the NationsBank Center in Houston. The sophisticated design of the building, with the elegant alternation between contrasting materials on the façade, is nonetheless characteristic of the care taken by this architect in choosing even the smallest details.

143 ■ The Lipstick Building breaks with Manhattan's rigid orthogonal grid and the nearby buildings, which are all characterized by right angles. This gives an almost tactile softness to the structure, justifying its whimsical name.

LOCATION	PROJECT	HEIGHT	MATERIALS	COMPLETION DATE
NEW YORK (U.S.A.)	JOHNSON/BURGEE ARCHITECTS	453 FT.	STEEL, ALUMINUM, AND GRANITE	1986

144 ■ The Lipstick Building's unusual shape is determined by two factors: the search for aesthetic innovations and the obligation to meet building regulations that require skyscrapers to "obscure" the street level as little as possible.

145 ■ The façade is seen here reflected in an adjacent building. It has a continuous curtain-wall consisting of enameled granite, steel, and ribbon windows with gray frames in alternation.

shape was not only determined by figurative forms but also by the zone's architectural regulations that, among others, prescribe the three successive setbacks toward the top that allow a greater quantity of light to reach the street below. Moreover, the elliptical plan of the building leaves a greater area of unoccupied ground space to be used by the public, and this is a valuable boon given the high density of people on Third Avenue. At the base, the tower stands on columns through which one passes to reach a vast, post-modern hall. This is a huge, hollow space as the elevators and emergency stairs are located in the rear of the building, where there is an enlargement of six more rectangular stories. Overall, the reinforced concrete structure is fairly traditional. It is composed of a sequence of inner columns strengthened by a core containing the elevators and stairwells, with a ring of outer columns connected by horizontal girders to absorb the horizontal loads. The structure is completely hidden behind a continuous curtain-wall of alternating horizontal bands of enameled granite, steel, and ribbon windows with gray frames. Another extraordinary and innovative feature of this building is that as the light hits the surface differently across the curvature of the building, it creates unusual effects and reflects the buildings all around it.

Rialto Towers

Built in the form of pure prisms and faced with a glass curtain-wall, the Rialto Towers are also based on the concept of duality, like the Twin Towers in New York, Marina City Towers in Chicago, and the later Petronas Towers in Kuala Lumpur and Emirates Twin Towers in Dubai. They belong to the generation of "late-modern Mannerist" designs that use an unidentifiable technology while betting everything on sheer height to make the building a recognizable and distinctive feature of the city skyline. Their glass facing reflects the changing colors of the sky to such an extent that one tends to lose sight of the volumes of the towers, which dematerialize into the general view of the city. The lower tower, the North Tower, is 43 stories high and 607 feet tall, whereas the higher tower, the South Tower, at 63 stories high and 824 feet tall, is still today one of the tallest buildings in the southern hemisphere. The prism shape of the tower gives way only at the top where there is a public observatory indicated from the outside by a loggia. For visitors to the city wishing to enjoy the superb view of the city and ocean, the observatory is an obligatory stop. Modern Melbourne is laid out on a rigid orthogonal grid at the center of which stand the towers. The city was founded in 1835 by John Barman, a rich merchant who landed in this area and bought roughly 620,000 acres of land from the indige-

146 ■ The Rialto Towers, seen in the foreground, stand out in the Melbourne skyline for their height. The grid of wide, straight streets that characterizes the city contributes greatly to the livability of the area.

147 ■ The reflective glass lining renders the volume of the towers imperceptible and softens its contrast with the prevalently Victorian-style buildings surrounding it. On one hand, it limits the visual impact of the building. On the other, it radically defines its style.

148 and 149 ▪ The base of the Rialto Towers is around ten stories high and features a large entrance atrium covered by a steel and glass roof. Various floors face onto the atrium, its shops, and public areas.

150-151 ▪ As these two photos taken respectively in the morning and at dusk illustrate, the towers have had a great impact on the skyline of Melbourne, a city that long remained in second place after Sydney but that has become a cosmopolitan center of primary importance for the Australia's economy.

nous people in return for a few provisions. Following the discovery of gold, many people moved there in search of fortune, the more successful of whom formed an upper-class colonial society. Grown wealthy on gold, they built luxurious Victorian-style houses that can still be seen in the area around the towers. On Collins Street in the city center, where there were many such buildings, it was decided during the 1970s to demolish many of them to make space for new constructions such as the Rialto Tower in order to give the city a more modern image. Today Collins Street is part of the central commercial district and the two towers have become an important point of reference in this part of the city. They contain 3,531,450 square feet of offices, a hotel, recreational facilities, an observatory with a bar on the 55th floor, and three underground floors of parking for 612 cars. The towers, made from reinforced concrete, brilliantly demonstrated their antiseismic properties when, during a strong earthquake in Newcastle in 1985, they did not suffer any damage.

Location	Project	Height	Materials	Completion date
Melbourne (Australia)	Gerard de Preu and Partners	824 ft.	Reinforced concrete and glass	1986

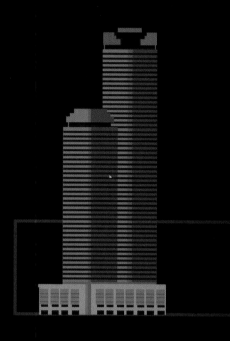

Liberty Place

T he Liberty Place complex in Philadelphia is composed of two towers made from the same materials and similar in style and the form of the roofs, yet the two are not identical twins. The higher of the two reaches a height of 945 feet, whereas the lower stops at 845 feet. Nonetheless, these towers are the tallest buildings in Philadelphia and all of Pennsylvania. Construction began when the City Council, in encouraging the construction of tall buildings along Market Street, gave permission for buildings to exceed the height of the statue of William Penn – founder of the city – that stands on top of City Hall at a combined elevation of 492 feet. Completed between 1987 and 1990 (the second tower was erected three years after the first) and standing at the intersection of Market Street and 17th Street, the two towers radically changed the city's image. Both towers were designed to hold offices, among them the world headquarters of Cigna Corporation, which is located in the first tower. The complex also includes a shopping mall and a luxury hotel. They were both designed by the German-born architect Helmut Jahn (since become an American citizen), an admirer of American Eclec-

152 ■ The top of One Liberty Place, the taller of the two towers of Liberty Place, resembles the Chrysler Building, one of New York's most famous skyscrapers. However, if it had been built in the 1920s or 30s, it would have probably taken double the amount of steel to build it.

153 ■ The Liberty Place towers respectively stand 945 and 847 feet high. Since their construction, they have radically changed the image of the city due to their height and their appearance.

154 top ■ Like other towers of the same period, the two towers, built three years apart, are not identical twins, even though they bear a strict resemblance. The structure of the roofs and the use of similar materials are also coordinating factors between the two buildings.

154 bottom ■ The overall appearance of the Liberty Place complex can be seen in the plan. Besides the two towers, there is also a shopping mall (in red) and a luxurious hotel (in green).

155 ■ The two skyscrapers have roofs with multiple faces and are quite unlike the other mostly flat-topped buildings in the commercial district.

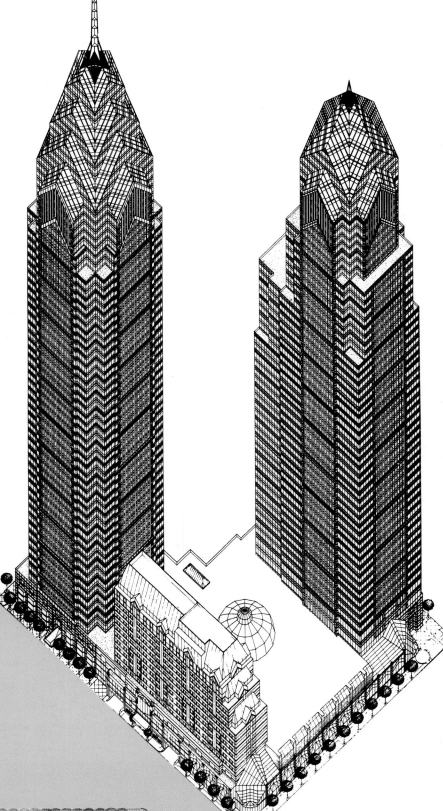

■ Offices

■ Stores

■ Hotel

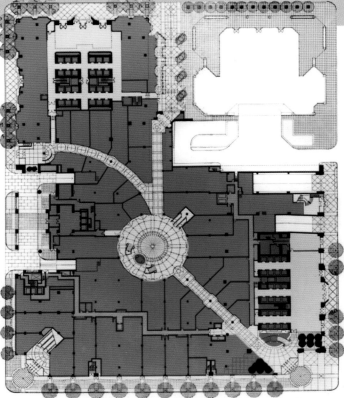

ticism and Art Deco of the 1920s and 30s, using his signature post-modern style featuring elements taken from architectural history. In this case, the principal reference is to one of the most famous New York skyscrapers, the Chrysler Building. Liberty Place features a square plan with recessed corners, three successive steps inwards at the top, and a terminal spar that, despite its angular lines, recalls the upper section of the Chrysler, from which it also copies the pinnacle at the top. Even the play of colors in the chromatics of the materials recalls the Chrysler, which are installed in horizontal bands at the cor-

Location	Project	Height	Materials	Completion date
Philadelphia (U.S.A.)	Murphy and Jahn	945 ft. and 847 ft.	Steel, aluminum, and glass	1987 and 1990

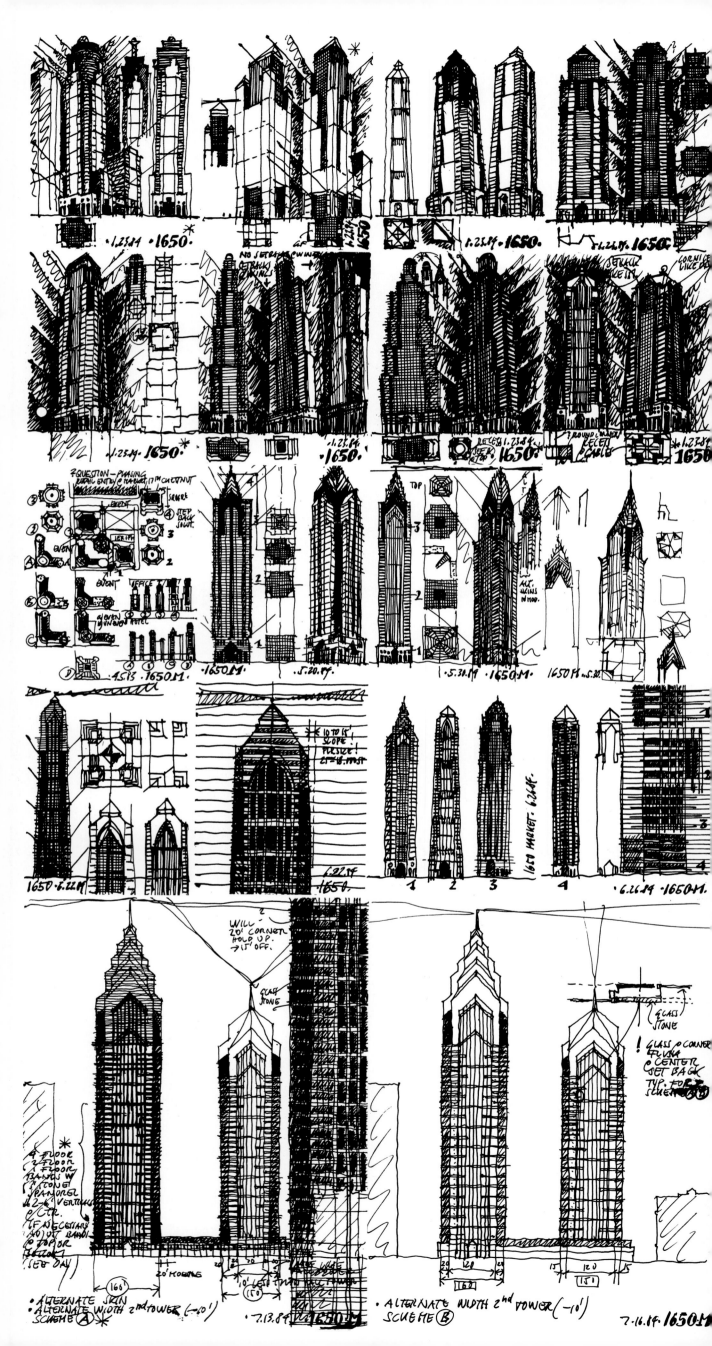

156 ■ These studio sketches illustrate the progress made in the building's conceptualization by German architect Jahn. Although the building is often compared to the Chrysler Building in New York, One Liberty Place has a much more imposing structure and a far more elaborately decorated crown.

157 ■ This illustration of the first tower emphasizes how it was modeled after William Van Alen's New York skyscraper. Both have a square plan with recessed corners, three successive setbacks at the top, and terminate in a spire. There is also a resemblance in the use of materials, with horizontal bands at the corners and vertical bands in the center of the façade.

ners and vertically in the center of the façade. Both the towers are characterized by an excessive, formalistic interlocking of solid geometric shapes in which the historic allusions to tympani, roofs, and spires are mingled with a practical exercise in crystallography. The towers have a steel structure formed by a central core containing the elevators and eight huge pillars around the perimeter. These are joined together to provide the structure with rigidity and to render the interior spaces as free as possible for the maximum flexibility in the office spaces. The exterior of the bottom levels as well as the multifloor atrium are lined with stone, while the rest of the building is lined with a "skin" of aluminum and glass panels. Toward the top, the quantity of glass increases. The second tower is not very different in appearance, also based on a rectangular plan to create more internal space, but the exterior looks slightly squatter and less elegant.

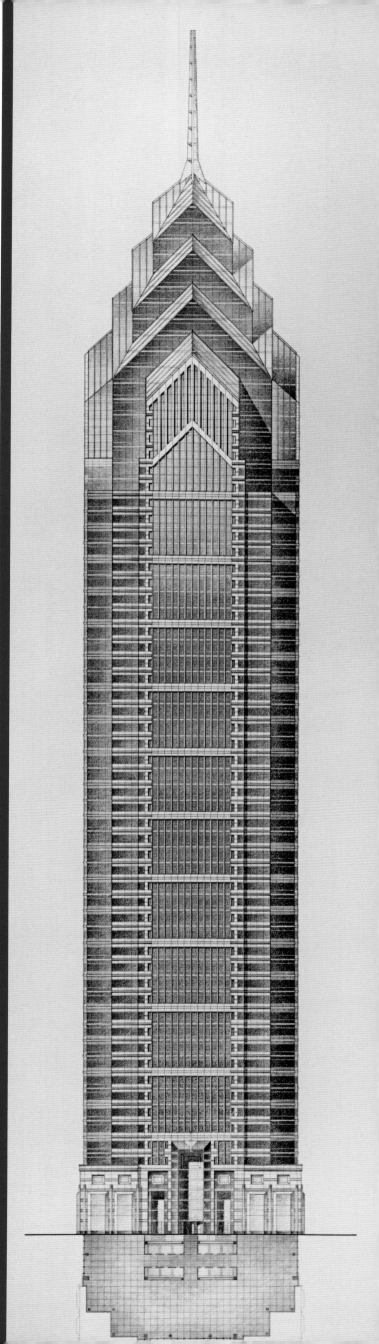

158 top ■ The exterior of the two skyscrapers is lined with aluminum and glass panels, with the glass increasing proportionately toward the top.

158 center ■ The drawing shows the base that connects the towers. It is lined with stone on the outside.

158 bottom and 159 ■ Various floors face onto the round atrium. It is a sort of inside public space with a huge glass skylight.

160-161 ■ Seen at night, the two towers of Liberty Place tower over Philadelphia, framing the statue of William Penn, the founder of the city.

161 right ■ The refined geometric design of One Liberty Place plays on the contrast between metal and glass, recalling characteristics typical of Art Deco.

Bank of China

Bank of China

Bank of China

Along with many other buildings, the bizarre shapes of Foster's Hong Kong and Shanghai Bank and Pei's Bank of China building are features in the Hong Kong skyline, but they differ from the rest in that their appearance is characterized by the use of advanced technologies. This renders them immediately recognizable and visible, as well as making them symbolic of the city's worldwide economic power and of the complexity of Hong Kong as a metropolis. Characteristic features of the urban area are limited available space for service industries, a highly congested infrastructure, and strong winds. The eccentric form of Pei's building is composed of a complex polygonal volume composed of tetrahedrons, a triangular prism at the top, and two antennas that rise from the roof. Pei had designed a similar form for the First Interstate Bank building in Dallas in 1986. The idea to build a new headquarters for the State Bank of the People's Republic of China was first conceived in 1984 when the city was still a British colony. The building, therefore, had an enormous symbolic value as it represented both the growing economic power of China and the reunification of this last foreign enclave with the motherland, which took place in 1997. For this reason, the Bank of

162 ■ The polygonal volume of tetrahedrons in Pei's skyscraper is best appreciated from the bottom. The tetrahedrons interact at different heights, getting smaller as they rise to the top, where the volume turns into a triangular prism.

163 ■ At night, the skyscraper, with its illuminated windows, partly loses its disembodied form, appearing as a single unit that blends into and almost resembles the other buildings in the city.

164 bottom right ■ The internal open space is enclosed by a skylight.

165 ■ Pei's skyscraper has a slender, immaterial form due partly to the use of aluminum cladding, which makes the structural elements seem even more slender than they really are.

China skyscraper stands at the center of the Hong Kong commercial district and, being the tallest, dominates the panorama. It is linked to Chinese tradition through the use of a structure analogous to bamboo cane (symbolizing the process of growth and progress in Eastern culture), and through the inclusion of an triangular-shaped park area in the three-story monumental granite base recalling ancient Chinese gardens. Exploiting the slope, small waterfalls and fountains enliven the area and create a quiet space in net contrast to the confusion of the district immediately outside; in fact, right at the base of the skyscraper new roads and highways are being built. Perhaps the most interesting feature of this building lies in its structure: not simply because it determines both the plan and façade, but also because, being slender (its aluminum lining tends to create an optical effect in which vertical elements seem slimmer), it succeeds in resolving all static problems posed by earthquakes, strong tropical winds, and the building's height. The structure stands on four enormous corner pylons made from concrete and steel. Diagonal girders connect them so that the internal space is free from structural ele-

164 top ■ The transportation and assembly of the structural elements (in this case parts of the antenna) during construction required a combination of high technology and personal courage.

164 bottom left ■ The floor in the atrium is made of differently colored marbles that create geometrical shapes.

Location	Project	Height	Materials	Completion date
Hong Kong (China)	I. M. Pei & Partners	1,204 ft.	Steel, concrete, aluminum, granite, and glass	1990

166-167 ■ **Though the city
bristles with skyscrapers, the
Bank of China stands out in
the Hong Kong panorama
thanks to its slender and
technological profile.**

ments. The same thing occurs on the façade: the system of squares crossed by diagonals creates a gigantic frame that provides wind resistance and transfers the horizontal forces first to the roof and then onto the four pylons.

There is a fifth central pillar in the upper section of the skyscraper where the two diagonals cross. Communication between the upper structure with five supports and the lower structure with four supports is furnished by a pyramidal module that conveys the forces from the central pillar along its edges, transferring them and dividing them among

the four perimeter pillars. This distinction between the upper and lower sections is also
functional. The lower part of the building contains the offices of the Bank of China whereas the upper section has been rented out to
other companies. The two are separated by
the sky-lobby on the 17th floor, where there is
a restaurant with a bar under the triangular
glass element that closes the first segment
of the volume. The volume is constituted by
five modules of equal height placed one over
the other, except for the apex and base (half

a module) for functional and structural reasons. The base, where the strain is greatest
but where there are no horizontal forces, has
a greater number of secondary pillars. In net
contrast with the effect of lightness and
transparency in the upper section of the
building, the granite lining on the lower floors
simulates a natural out-cropping anchored to
the ground. In addition, the skyscraper has
purposely been invested with references to
architectural history in order to give it a monumental appearance.

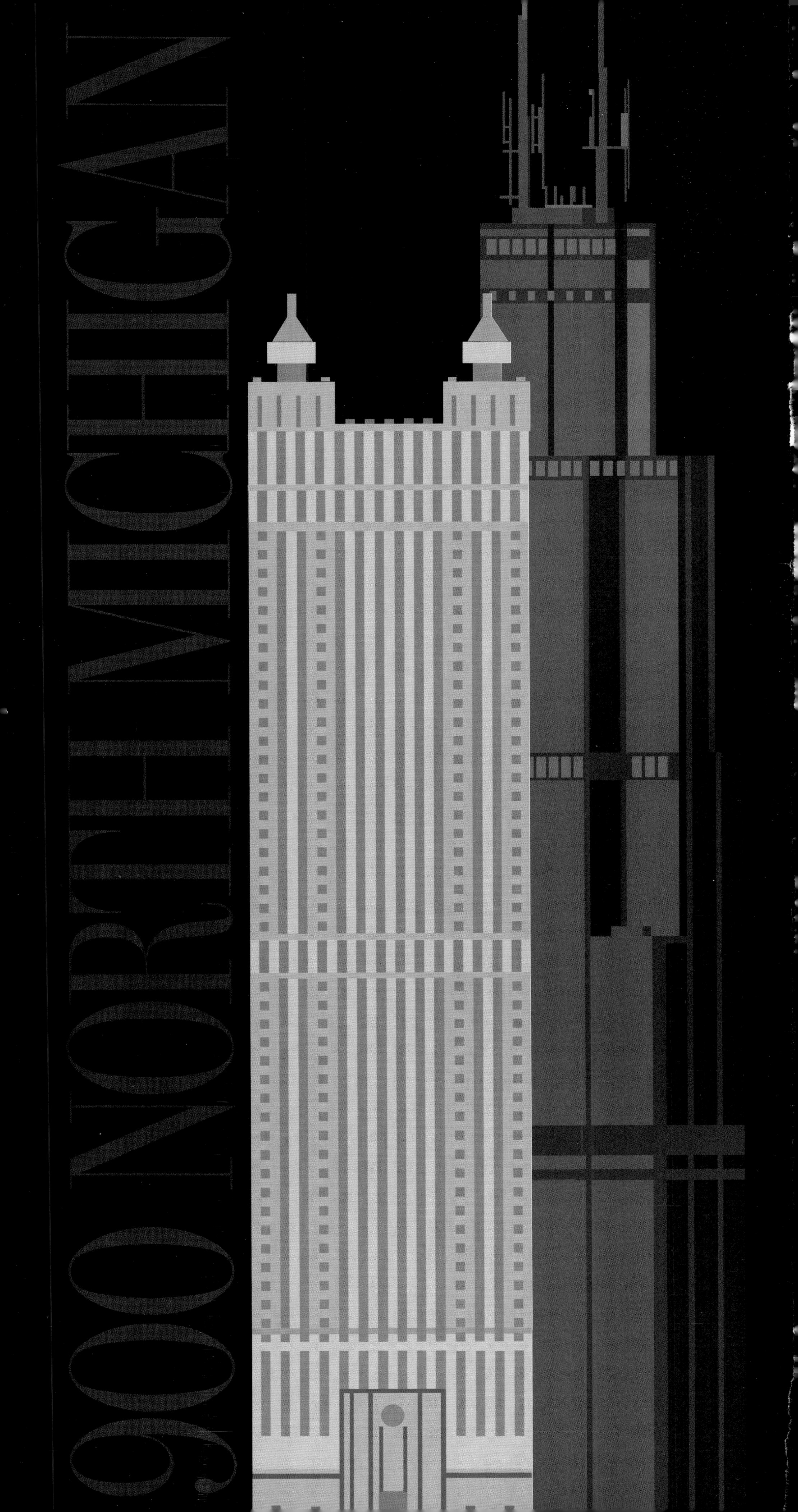
900 NORTH MICHIGAN

900 North Michigan

900 North Michigan is a multifunctional building of 66 stories that contains offices, a shopping mall, a hotel with 340 rooms, 19 apartments, and parking for 1,710 cars. It is located on Michigan Avenue in downtown (Near North) Chicago. This street is famous for its prestigious shops and is lined on either side by low buildings whose richly decorated façades give a uniformly elegant and pleasing appearance, hence the street's nickname of The Magnificent Mile. The construction of the new, multifunctional building in 1989 only increased the prestige of this street in the city.

The design by Kohn Petersen Fox was appreciated for the continuity it created with the existing buildings, which it succeeded in doing by assimilating some of their typical characteristics. Although the new building is 869 feet high, it manages to create a rapport of scale with its neighbors through its eight-story base. It is lined with granite, marble, and cream-colored limestone, and is decorated with moldings in the style of the buildings next to it, which are also faced with different types of stone. The Michigan Avenue side of the base features a large doorway that leads into the six-story atrium where there is a shopping mall and the large

168 ■ The continuity between 900 North Michigan and adjacent buildings was created by using the same materials and repeating the division of the building into a base, shaft, and crown.

169 ■ The vertical three-part façade is lined with granite, marble, and limestone. It has vertical rows of windows in the center to give a continuous line, while the slightly sloped sides feature the same windows framed by wider bands in which the openings create horizontal designs.

LOCATION	PROJECT	HEIGHT	MATERIALS	COMPLETION DATE
CHICAGO (U.S.A.)	KOHN PEDERSEN FOX ASSOCIATES, PERKINS AND WILL GROUP	869 FT.	STEEL, GRANITE, MARBLE, LIMESTONE, AND GLASS	1989

170 left ■ Inside the base there is a 59-foot-high atrium onto which the shopping mall faces. It also gives access to the large entrance hall to the Chicago Four Seasons Hotel.

170 right ■ The illustration of the south side shows how both the base, which reflects the style of the surrounding buildings, and the façade, with the play of full and empty spaces, were designed using an alternation of different types of windows.

170-171 ■ The importance and name of 900 North Michigan are due to its location on Michigan Avenue, a central street lined with prominent stores and elegant buildings that has earned it the nickname "The Magnificent Mile."

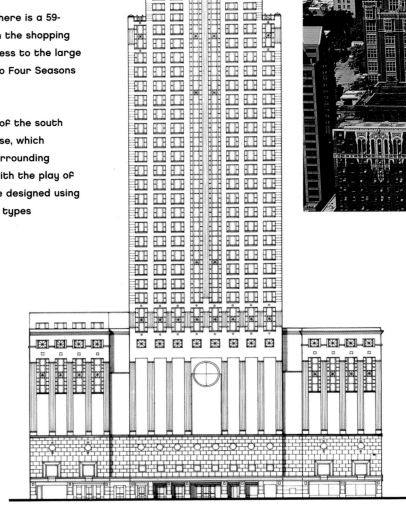

entrance hall to the Chicago Four Seasons Hotel.

The new building also managed to create a link with its surroundings by repeating the division characteristic of older buildings into a base, tower, and crown. In addition, typical of Chicago, the façade is continuously lined at the corners to give an image of mass and unity, but it has slender vertical stripes in the center to give the building a sense of slimness. Similarly, the windows are larg-

er in the center but narrower toward the sides. Beneath the facing materials, the structure has a steel frame. Contributing to the sense of slenderness, a sequence of steps retreats inward along the façade as it reaches the top of the tower. Each one corresponds to a functional division of the building: the shopping mall in the base, the offices in the middle section, and the hotel and residences in the upper part. The building terminates in four small towers, one on

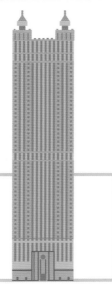

each corner, which are lit up at night and, during the Christmas season, with changing colors.

The initial design was provided with a dome at the top, similar to the one designed by Otto Wagner in Vienna during the Secession Period. Although the idea was abandoned, 900 North Michigan remains redolent with rich decoration and elements borrowed from architectural history, giving the building a Post-Modern character.

172-173 ■ The skyscraper makes its presence felt at night thanks to the top with its four lantern-style towers. Like the rest of the building, the historical references of the towers express tastes typical of Post-Modern style.

Two Prudential Plaza

Prudential Plaza in Chicago was designed for offices. It consists of two towers, the first of which was built in 1955 and the second in 1987. It stands in an area enclosed by four busy streets, one of which, North Stetson Avenue, flanks Grant Park, which runs for a mile and a half along Lake Michigan. Thanks to this location, the tower enjoys a superb view over Michigan Avenue, the park, and the lake. Today this area is the gateway to the commercial district, though historically it was occupied by the railroad, which made it rather difficult to obtain the land and the rights to build the first skyscraper.

The first tower, One Prudential Plaza, erected in 1955, was Chicago's tallest building for ten years and one of the most modern constructions of the postwar period with its 41 stories standing 600 feet tall. It had 30 automatic elevators (then the fastest in the world), double-glazed windows, a modern air-conditioning system, and one of the largest parking lots built within an office building. For many years, it was one of the city's greatest tourist attractions, thanks to the restaurant at the top and the observation deck on the

174 ■ Like its façades, Two Prudential Plaza's pyramidal roof features alternating bands of granite and reflective glass, which form arrow-shaped patterns on the sides, making the tower unmistakable in the Chicago skyline. In the corners, further space was created for offices, with particular attention paid to the demands of the real-estate market typical of big American cities.

175 ■ The unique profile of the pyramidal roof of Two Prudential Plaza is dominated by the imposing square silhouette of the former Amoco Building (now the AON Center), Chicago's second tallest building.

176 center ■ The drawing shows the 1980s development plan for the area, which included the rebuilding of One Prudential Plaza, the creation of a new 64-story skyscraper, and a large piazza with an atrium connecting the two towers.

176 bottom ■ The large, five-story atrium that connects the towers offers a splendid view of the square, Grant Park, and Michigan Avenue thanks to its abundant use of glass.

177 ■ Prudential Plaza is surrounded by four large streets and stands near Grant Park, an immense green area along Lake Michigan.

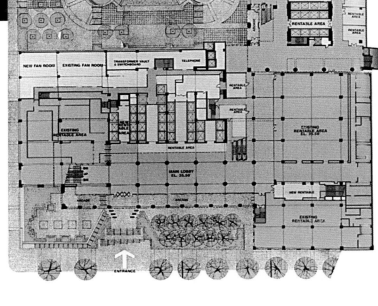

176 top ■ The square in front of the Two Prudential Plaza features fountains and trees and provides visitors with benches where they can take a break from the big city's frenetic lifestyle.

Location	Project	Height	Materials	Completion date
Chicago (U.S.A.)	Loebl, Schlossman & Hackl	994 ft.	Reinforced concrete, aluminum, and limestone	1990

41st floor. Two years after its opening in 1956 it had already received a million visitors.

Thirty years later, the Prudential Property Company decided to renovate the area where One Prudential Plaza stood through a development plan that included the remodeling of the existing skyscraper, the creation of a new 64-floor tower, and a large square lying between the two towers. These were united by an atrium and shared the same decoration scheme. The square was landscaped with flower gardens in addition to two fountains, seating, and trees in the north corner where pedestrians could rest and cool themselves.

Remodeling the first tower required the cleaning of the façades. These are decorated with vertical strips of aluminum and limestone and embellished with limestone sculptures by Alfonzo Ianelli, designer of the Rock of Gibraltar, the company's symbol. Modern equipment was installed for heating, air-conditioning, safety, lighting, and elevator systems, and decorative elements added to the walls, the ceilings, and elevator doors. The most remarkable feature, however, is the huge, five-story atrium connecting Tower One to Tower Two. Not only does it provide easy access to the AON Center, but it also

178-179 ■ The roof of Two Prudential Plaza (the more recent of the two towers) is a pyramid with an octagonal base and a spectacular spire. The tower does not at all resemble Tower One, built 30 years earlier, and purposely breaks with the typical "box" concept of the skyscraper popular until the 1970s.

affords a splendid view of the square, Grant Park, and Michigan Avenue, thanks to the abundant use of glass walls at street level.

Tower Two was built in 1987 and soon became a new symbolic element in the Chicago skyline, owing to its visible nature and 994 feet height. Its volume is created by a parallelepiped on a square base with successive cutbacks toward the top as far as its octagonal-pyramid covering. The main sides of the pyramid cut the prism to give a "crystalline" continuity with the sheath of the building. Its façades cover a reinforced-concrete structure and are characterized at the sides by alternating vertical strips of gray and pink granite and reflecting gray glass. In the center, there is a continuous wall made of reflecting glass, and the façades to the north and south feature a series of zigzagging recesses. The roof follows the same alternating bands of granite and glass at the sides down to the upper part of the zigzagging façades. The central section, on the other hand, features a granite gabled roof that matches the glass curtain-wall.

Library Tower

At over 1,000 feet tall, the Library Tower of the First Interstate World Center is a landmark in the center of Los Angeles, despite the fact that it stands among many tall skyscrapers of original design. It stands in a central district that has no particularly high-quality architectural sights except for the central library, which was built in 1926 by the architect Bertram Grosvenor Goodhue. Merger Thomas Partners, the tower's promoter, procured the rights from the City Council to move the library to the other side of the street to allow the tower's construction. With the money from the sale of the rights, the city administration restored and modernized the library, which had been heavily damaged by a fire in the 1970s.

Event the most severe critics perceived strong architectural links between the tower and library. As with the John Hancock Tower in Boston, where the architect established a close relationship with the charming Trinity Church, here an esthetic connection with the library was sought. The link was formed by the layout of the tower at ground level, where the landscape architect Lawrence Halprin designed Bunker Hill Steps (inspired by the Spanish Steps in Rome), a reconstruction of a cable railway connecting two elevations in the district that terminates at the foot of the library.

180 ■ Library Tower, seen here reflected in an adjacent building, is situated in the business district of Los Angeles, a city characterized by an extensive spread of low buildings.

181 ■ The tower of the First Interstate World Center is known as Library Tower in Los Angeles. It has a bizarre shape created by the intersection of parallelepipeds and cylinders crowned by a round section.

The form of the tower is based on the overlaying of two geometrical figures, rectangles, and circles, combined in a variety of ways, until the last five stories where the form is simply circular. The structure is of particular importance as the site lies just 25 miles from the San Andreas fault. It was designed to withstand an earthquake measuring 8.3 on the Richter scale as well as to resist the strength of the wind. At 1,017 feet, the First Interstate World Center is the tallest building in an earthquake zone.

The load-bearing structure is composed of a dual cage formed by a central core containing twenty-two elevators, two emergency stairwells, and the building's facilities. Around this core lies the ductile exterior "skin." It absorbs most of the building's loads, as well as the horizontal forces created by the wind transmitted through the floors. This allows the pillars toward the outer part of the building to be slender and hollow. The core structure means that the offices enjoy an open space in which there is no further need of bulky structural components. From the 53rd floor up, the horizontal forces created by the wind and earthquakes are absorbed by two struts, each a floor high. Further up the central structure is composed by a frame strengthened in two directions. The terminal section of the building, where there are no load problems,

Location	Project	Height	Materials	Completion date
Los Angeles (U.S.A.)	Pei Cobb Freed & Partners	1,017 ft.	Steel, granite, and glass	1990

has been designed as a glass crown that is lit up at night. The façade is entirely lined with light granite strips alternating with rectangular windows each 21 feet in length. These emphasize the verticality of the building, which is only interrupted by three large horizontal cuts at the 48th, 57th, and 69th floors. The façade too has been designed to absorb deformation caused by earthquakes of up to two and a half inches per floor without any danger of collapse. As Mario Campi says, "The First Interstate World Center appears a symbol of grace, power, and resistance," even though it was one of the buildings destroyed by aliens in the 1997 film *Independence Day*.

182-183 ■ At 1,017 feet tall and bizarrely shaped, Library Tower has become a reference point in the central business district of Los Angeles.

183 right ■ The façade is lined with light granite slabs measured by series of wide, rectangular windows. Three horizontal bands of big windows placed at different heights create a break in the otherwise uniform surface.

Messeturm

Although the Messeturm was Europe's tallest building when it was completed in 1990, Norman Foster's Commerzbank, also in Frankfurt, topped it in 1997. These two buildings, together with the DZ Bank tower at 682 feet, the 1,086-foot-tall Europaturm television tower, and other skyscrapers in the city center have changed not just the skyline but also the layout of the city.

Frankfurt is perhaps the only city in Europe that accepts the construction of tall buildings not only on its outskirts but also in its city center. Skyscrapers are not considered just as isolated, random constructions but as a constellation of disparate forms and dimensions symbolizing the city's great economic and financial growth.

The Messeturm is situated in the Messe Frankfurt, a large exhibition area in the center of the city. It stands close to the entrance pavilion and the new Exhibition Hall 1 that forms the entrance to the Messeturm itself, a role that is emphasized by the gateway design of its base. The architect was Helmut Jahn, German by birth but American by adoption, and thus he is well versed with the works of Mies van der Rohe. He terms the overall shape of the tower "anthropomorphic" in the sense that it has an upper section

184 ■ The final section of the Messeturm features the overlapping of a cylinder and pyramid, both lined with a curtain-wall of steel, glass, and red granite.

185 ■ The Messeturm was designed by Helmut Jahn, German by birth but American by adoption, and a disciple of Mies van der Rohe. The tower, with its slim, bell-tower-shaped profile, is a management center and a point of interest in the Fair zone of Frankfurt.

Ground Floor

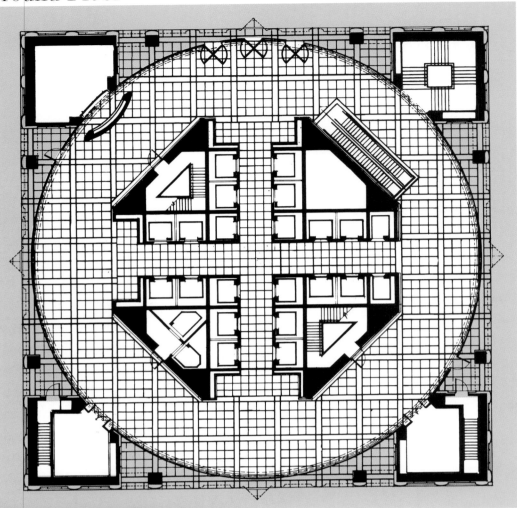

Messeturm

186 top ■ The plans feature the intersection of a cylinder and four squares that together mirror the square at the base, inside which the emergency stairwells are contained within an octagon constituting the central core.

186 bottom ■ The Messeturm stands at the entrance to the Frankfurt Fair, a huge exposition complex in the center of the city. Its imposing base lined in red granite with stripes of horizontal aluminum bands actually functions as the entrance to one of the pavilions.

187 ■ The glass cylinder atrium (seen here from the inside) adds to the "monumental" role of the tower entrance. The Fair's management offices are housed in the upper section of the tower.

made up of several distinct parts distinguished as a base, a vertical element, and a crown. This concept contrasts with the abstract geometrical forms of van der Rohe's skyscrapers. Jahn's vision was highly influenced by Eclecticism and Art Deco of the 1920s and 30s, styles that led to the construction of famous skyscrapers like the Woolworth Building and the Chrysler Building in the United States. In the same way, Jahn wanted to design a building that reestablished a relationship with history, could be distinguished from the "container" buildings typical of modern cities, was formed by several overlapping elements, and made use of avant-garde technologies. The tower rests

Location	Project	Height	Materials	Completion date
Frankfurt (Germany)	Murphy and Jahn	843 ft.	Steel, red granite, and glass	1990

188 ■ Jahn's drawings show the refined decoration of the outside of the tower, purposely chosen to link it to the architectural style of Frankfurt, a city in which many public buildings are distinguished by the color red, even if they are faced with materials other than granite.

on a cubic base and then rises in a parallelepiped from which the edges have been erased for almost all its height. On top of this stands a cylinder and, finally, a pyramid. The cylinder on the parallelepiped in the upper section is a reoccurring figure throughout the tower, reappearing in the curved glass that

Messeturm

gives access to the atrium in the base.

The structure is made from reinforced cement and is lined by a curtain-wall of steel, glass, and red granite. The red granite slabs are cut very thin in such a way as to be inserted into the steel structure to form prefabricated panels. These are then attached onto steel supports grafted directly onto the concrete.

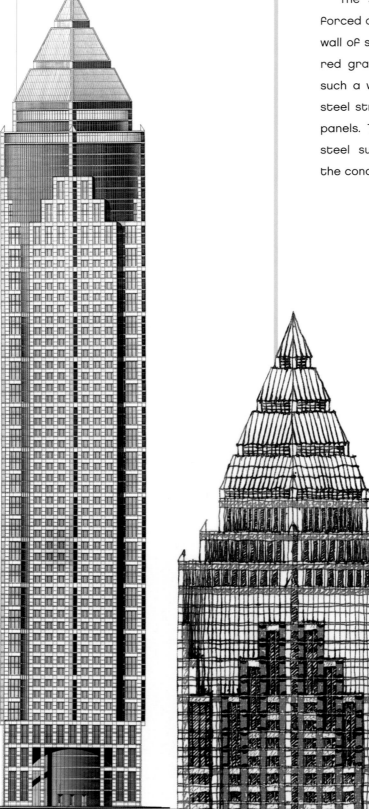

189 ■ These sketches show the Messeturm and other skyscrapers designed by the German architect Jahn. Formed by three distinct parts, the tower has an anthropomorphic shape that highlights the classical division into a base, vertical section, and crown.

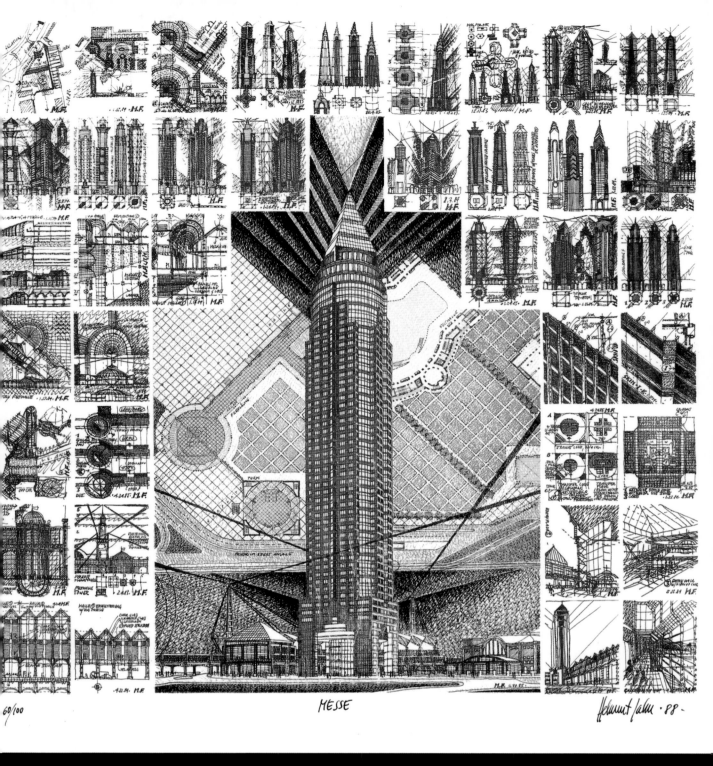

60/100   MESSE   Helmut Jahn · 88 ·

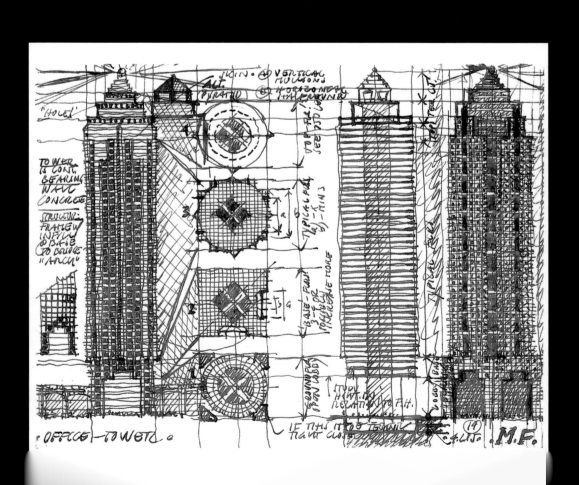

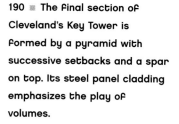

Key Tower

he tallest building in Cleveland and Ohio, one of the tallest in all of the United States, the tallest between Chicago and New York, and among the tallest 50 in the world, the Key Tower can be seen from up to twenty miles away. This tower is located in downtown Cleveland close to the business district, near the Burnham and Root Society For Savings Bank, and between two of the city's most important public spaces, Public Square and the Mall. The BP American Tower and the Terminal Tower are both located in the Mall, the latter of which was the city's tallest building before the construction of Key Tower.

It was financed by the R.E. Jacobs Group and was initially named the Society Center, but this was changed when the company was purchased by the Key Corporation. The design was conceived by the famous American architect Cesar Pelli and very much resembles the first proposal he made for another skyscraper, the Norwest Tower, built three years earlier in Minneapolis. In its unmistakable post-modern style, the Key Tower is a traditional, late twentieth-century construction on a rectangular plan, above which rises

190 ■ The final section of Cleveland's Key Tower is formed by a pyramid with successive setbacks and a spar on top. Its steel panel cladding emphasizes the play of volumes.

191 ■ The monumental Key Tower, with its pure form ending in a pyramid, is the tallest building in Cleveland, visible from 20 miles away.

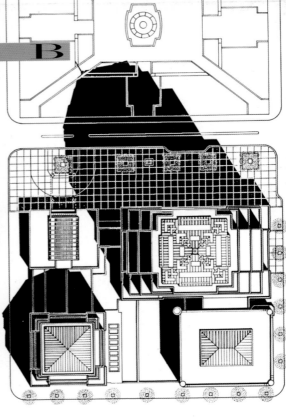

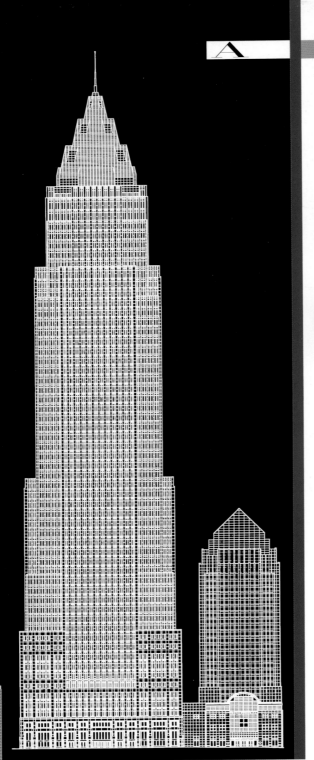

192 top ■ The various buildings are all rectangular in plan (B): the tower, an earlier brick building, a lower tower (also designed by Pelli), and a three-story building covered by a glass barrel vault. The link with the adjoining brick building is created by the stone-lined base and all the buildings are joined by passages concealed from the outside (A).

192 in bottom ■ Key Tower is situated in downtown Cleveland between two of the most important public areas: Public Square and the Mall, where the BP American Tower and Terminal Tower also stand.

Location	Project	Height	Materials	Completion date
Cleveland (U.S.A.)	Cesar Pelli	948 ft.	Reinforced concrete and steel	1991

a parallelepiped volume that gradually cuts back as the height increases. The top is formed by a pyramid that also retreats until reaching a spar at the top. The base is faced with stone so as to create a link with the brick building beside it, lined with brick facing. This too is part of the complex, and the two are connected by a passageway hidden from the outside. The upper part of the tower is lined with steel panels.

The composite structure is formed by a steel skeleton around the perimeter in addition to a central core that, apart from bearing the building's loads, houses the elevators and facilities.

193 ■ The tower is based on a parallelepiped that retreats as it rises and is characterized by the regular pattern of its windows.

Tokyo City Hall

In November 1985, the city authorities in Tokyo decided to announce a closed competition for the construction of a new City Hall as the old one was considered obsolete and no longer able to provide the services required by such a large and modern city. The offices in the old building in the district of Marunouchi had been expanded at random with a series of disconnected buildings. The purpose of the competition was to incorporate all the administrative functions within one complex, endowed with structures able to accommodate even international conference facilities, research centers, and technical offices, as a symbol of the expansion of a metropolis that was home to thirteen million people at the time.

The site chosen for the new offices was Shinjuku, where three areas were owned by the city. The purpose of this choice was that the new building would be part of a larger urban project, which included, among others, a large, public square dedicated to the gathering and meeting of citizens. Nine architects were approached to submit their ideas, and in April 1986 Kenzo Tange's proposal was announced the winner. The design was based on two main towers: the first contains the offices of the governor and is 48 stories high, but at the 33rd floor it divides into twin towers that each reach a height of 797 feet. The second tower is 33 stories high and contains the public offices, departments, and

194 ■ The façade of Tokyo City Hall is lined in aluminum and has patterns resembling electronic circuits to give the building a "technological" look.

195 ■ The new City Hall complex comprises two main buildings: the 48-story higher tower branches into two twin towers that reach 797 feet and the 33-story lower tower that is divided into three elements of different heights.

various agencies. In the upper section of the second tower there are three parts of different heights placed in descending order, with the lowest one closest to the first tower. In addition to the towers, the complex includes the Assembly Building in front of the first tower and the semi-elliptical square that forms the central axis of the entire district, which can hold 6,000 people. A park lies behind the first tower. Being an architect attentive to urban space, Tange tries to emphasize public functions, and thus the square plays a fundamental role in allowing people to come together and communicate. A series of connections between the towers at the third floor united the towers that are also linked via the public infrastructures. Thus, access to the system is provided on two levels: the lower one for pedestrians at the

196-197 ■ The complex includes an oval public space at the foot of the taller tower surrounded by columns and embellished with abstract sculptures that can even host concerts.

196 bottom left ■ The interior has a series of levels linked by escalators.

196 bottom right ■ Access to the first tower from the square is indicated by a concrete cantilever roof lined with aluminum.

197 right ■ The Assembly Room in the building that encloses the square is oval, like the glass roof above.

level of the square, which joins the subway station to the lower floors of the City Hall, and the upper one for use by automobiles.

The first tower has a cross-shaped plan in which the elevators are located at the corners. Where the tower splits into two on floor 33, the plan switches to a square but is rotated so that the corners bisect those of the cross. The structure uses a module of 63-foot free spaces so that offices can be organized in an extremely flexible manner with mobile division walls and areas of greenery. The façade is completely lined with aluminum in the forms of traditional Japanese architecture, expressed through vertical and horizontal elements. A dense weave of figures recalling electronic circuits are superimposed over the historical forms to provide a modern technological image appropriate to the Japan of today.

Location	Project	Height	Materials	Completion date
Tokyo (Japan)	Kenzo Tange	797 ft.	Steel, granite, and aluminum	1991

Canary Wharf Tower

Canary Wharf is the largest commercial district ever built. It lies in the Docklands area about three miles from the center of London and is the first district in Great Britain to have skyscrapers. Canary Wharf is home to the country's three tallest buildings.

The tower is part of a large project to convert the previously abandoned Docklands area (in the past used for warehouses and industrial buildings linked to the port on the Thames) into a state-of-the-art financial and commercial district. The 1980s were characterized by the prevalence of post-modern style — a style approved of by Prince Charles — in which it was thought that by rebuilding parts of the city using an architectural language that makes use of historic elements in the city, it would find more favor with the public. Construction in the area began in 1988 but was stopped by the recession at the start of the 1990s. Then work started up again despite the objections of the local people who protested that prices in the area were being raised by the project, and that it was no longer within the reach of the traditional inhabitants, who were being replaced by companies and private individuals attracted to the prestige of the new complex.

Canary Wharf is divided into three main sections: a 50-story office tower officially named One Canada Square, the Retail and Assembly Building, and the rail link station. Set on the second floor and connected to the tower via a walkway, the station is covered by a glass and steel vault similar in

198 ■ The corner view of One Canada Square shows the intersection of two parallelepipeds; the outer one, which forms the main façades, and the inner one that recreates the corners and forms the higher part of the building.

199 ■ Canary Wharf is designed in Post-Modern style using elements from the city's architectural history.

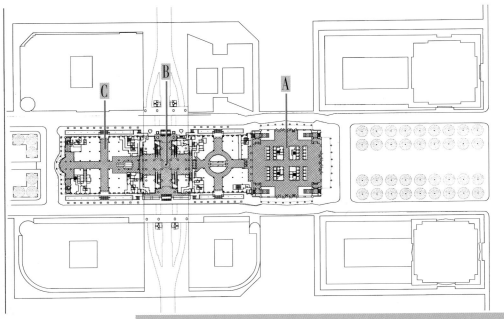

200-201 ■ Canary Wharf is an impressive new commercial district in the Docklands area that contains the United Kingdom's three tallest buildings.

200 bottom ■ The complex comprises three main parts: an office tower (A), the rail link station (B), and the Retail and Assembly Building (C). This last building has public spaces, exhibition space, and meeting rooms.

concept to the large nineteenth-century railway stations of London. The Retail and Assembly Building accommodates shops, restaurants, and public spaces, whereas the Assembly Hall contains meeting rooms and exhibition areas. The entire group of buildings is based on a symmetrical plan: the pure and monumental tower of One Canada Square, the tallest building in Great Britain, stands at the center. It is a four-sided prism with smoothed edges to give it a greater sense of thrust and a crown in the form of a pyramid. The American architect Cesar Pelli, accustomed to borrowing images from architectural history and inserting them in post-modern style, decided to use a form that resembles a monumental obelisk because, he states, "It is a form recognized by all cultures." Another element that recurs in Pelli's projects is the façade designed like a palace with alternations of horizontal and vertical rectangular windows that give the building a massive and imposing

Location	Project	Height	Materials	Completion date
LONDON (UNITED KINGDOM)	CESAR PELLI AND ASSOCIATES	774 FT.	STEEL AND STAINLESS STEEL	1991

201 bottom left ■ Seen in profile, the "palace"-style façade alternates rectangular windows with horizontal and vertical bands to give the building a more imposing appearance and make it resemble the enormous obelisk overlooking the River Thames.

201 bottom right ■ Taken during construction, the entirely steel structure can be plainly seen. Foundations are formed by 222 pylons, each about six feet in diameter and 66 feet deep. They are essential to the stability of the building because of the strong winds in this area.

202-203 ■ Lined completely in stainless steel, the façade reflects the London sky but does not diminish the impressive appearance of the building.

CANARY WHARF Tower

202 bottom ■ An tree-lined avenue at the base of the building forms a perspective line toward the façade. It is lined with fountains and statues to create a pleasant public space.

air. In this case, the façade is lined with stainless steel that reflects the changes in the London sky, but this does not diminish the building's image, which, thanks also to its dominant position on the river, appears nonetheless monumental.

The structure is made entirely from steel, including its foundations made from 222 pylons, each of which measures nearly six feet in diameter and burrows 66 feet into the ground. This anchoring system is particularly important as it confers solidity to the building that is essential in consideration of the strong winds that affect the area.

203 bottom ■ Seen from the River Thames, the pure form of the tower, with a four-sided prism crowned by a pyramid, stands out in its surroundings.

204-205 ■ The station is covered by a glass and steel vault like the great London stations of the nineteenth century.

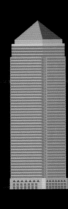

Bank of America

Bank of America Corporate Center

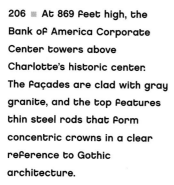

At a height of 869 feet, the Bank of America Corporate Center is the tallest tower in the southeastern United States. It stands in the historic center of Charlotte, which is also the city's financial district. The construction of this building had several objectives: to accommodate the bank's offices, to reach a record height, to be a local landmark, and to give a boost to the city center by fulfilling a series of both public and private social functions. To this end, the Bank of America Corporate Center complex, of which the tower is a part, contains the North Carolina Performing Arts Center, a hotel, panoramic squares, and Founder's Hall, a large public gallery that contains a shopping mall and other functions.

Located between Tryon Street and Fifth Street, the North Carolina Performing Arts Center consists of two theaters (one with 2,100 seats, and the other with 450) including their related facilities and a large, two-story, semicircular foyer covered by a glass skylight. The main entrance to the entire building is via Tryon Street, where the complex's base is lined with reddish-color granite to give it a feeling of solidity, and the entrance is emphasized by four black marble columns. Other entrances to the building are accessed via pedestrian bridges or under-

206 ▪ At 869 feet high, the Bank of America Corporate Center towers above Charlotte's historic center. The façades are clad with gray granite, and the top features thin steel rods that form concentric crowns in a clear reference to Gothic architecture.

207 ▪ The building is characterized by a series of setbacks as it rises, a common feature of some of the most important American skyscrapers of the golden era, which clearly were an important source of inspiration for the architect.

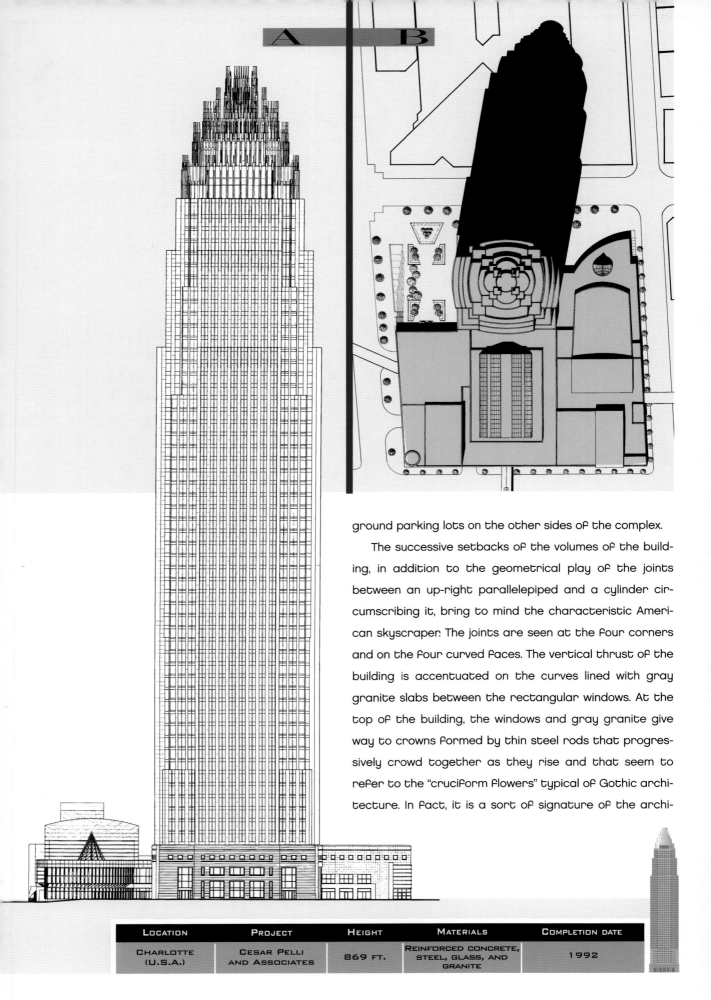

A B

LOCATION	PROJECT	HEIGHT	MATERIALS	COMPLETION DATE
CHARLOTTE (U.S.A.)	CESAR PELLI AND ASSOCIATES	869 FT.	REINFORCED CONCRETE, STEEL, GLASS, AND GRANITE	1992

ground parking lots on the other sides of the complex.

The successive setbacks of the volumes of the building, in addition to the geometrical play of the joints between an up-right parallelepiped and a cylinder circumscribing it, bring to mind the characteristic American skyscraper. The joints are seen at the four corners and on the four curved faces. The vertical thrust of the building is accentuated on the curves lined with gray granite slabs between the rectangular windows. At the top of the building, the windows and gray granite give way to crowns formed by thin steel rods that progressively crowd together as they rise and that seem to refer to the "cruciform flowers" typical of Gothic architecture. In fact, it is a sort of signature of the archi-

208 ■ As seen in the perspective (A) and layout (B) designs, the Bank of America Corporate Center is complex composed of many buildings, including the North Carolina Performing Arts Center and Founder's Hall, a large public gallery containing a shopping mall and other amenities.

209 ■ The lighting system shows off the setbacks of the curved walls and the almost glass-like evanescence of the concentric crowns, creating a powerful presence in Charlotte's skyline.

tect, Cesar Pelli, to combine the most advanced technologies with forms taken from architectural history in his works (World Financial Center in New York, Canary Wharf Tower in London, and Petronas Towers in Kuala Lumpur), thus creating post-modern images in which the public will find forms they recognize. This is in contrast to the pure crystal prisms typical of International Style.

The lighting system accentuates both the room vaulted with a transparent roof at the top of the skyscraper and the successive curved walls that step back as they rise, creating a remarkable effect at night, and allowing the building to dominate the city skyline, in which it constitutes an essential point of reference.

Central Plaza

Representative of an increasingly recurring form of architecture, Central Plaza is one of the new names often given to contemporary skyscrapers everywhere. The Central Plaza in Hong Kong, along with Citic Plaza in Guangzhou, is one of the tallest buildings in reinforced concrete in the world. Moreover, it was the highest in its city for a long time and the second highest in Asia after Shun Hing Square in Shenzhen. With 78 stories, Central Plaza is built in the shape of a triangular prism that culminates in a pyramid topped by a rod nearly 200 feet tall. Its profile characterizes the skyline and is best seen when arriving by sea, from where the city's "mountain of skyscrapers" is very visible, with Central Plaza soaring up to double the average height of the surrounding buildings. This skyscraper is typical of the Eastern constructions that combine an image of advanced technology with the iconography of the traditional skyscraper. Even its location contributes to the uniqueness of the building as it stands in front of the 591-foot-high Hong Kong Convention and Exhibition Center (HKCEC) and next to a 577-foot-high government office building on one side and a three-story fire-station on the other. Most importantly, it is surrounded by a tangle of wide streets, among which Gloucester Road, one of the largest in Hong Kong. At the base of the tower, there is a vast, paved pedestrian area

210 ■ Central Plaza combines futuristic technology with tradition, creating an innovative building though reassuringly similar in appearance to traditional buildings, in particular American skyscrapers. Surrounded by large roads and featuring a public space at its base connected to neighboring buildings via bridges, it is situated in a rather original urban context.

211 ■ Central Plaza rises above the Hong Kong metropolis. Its triangular base, pyramidal crown, and antenna have become a feature of the city skyline.

李錦記

212 top and 213 ■ The building is seen here toward the end of construction. Its reinforced concrete structure can be seen clearly. This material is cheaper than steel but limiting in terms of height.

212 bottom left ■
The three-part elevation (base, body, and top) is a relatively conventional design, ending in a pyramidal crown.

212 bottom right ■
The plan is formed by two concentric equilateral triangles, both structural and with smoothed corners. The internal polygon contains the elevators, stairwells, and facilities while the outer one contains the offices.

with a garden containing trees, fountains, and benches. The 100-foot-high bottom section of the building encompasses a public area and three pedestrian bridges that cross over heavily-trafficked roads to connect to the bases of the HKCEC, fire station, and the China Resource building, forming a raised, futuristic, science-fiction-like level. Above the base rise 57 stories of offices, an observatory level open to the public that gives splendid views over the bay and port, and five stories housing mechanical and energy equipment. The concept of an office building has been revolutionized with the addition of high-quality common areas, a swimming pool, a club, and a series of recreational activities. The tower has a plan formed by two concentric equilateral triangles. The outer one – with cut corners – rises in three parts to the point where the inner triangle joins the spire. The golden tubes of the inner triangle seem to grow right out of the corners of the base below.

LOCATION	PROJECT	HEIGHT	MATERIALS	COMPLETION DATE
HONG KONG (CHINA)	DENNIS LAU & N.G. CHUN MAN ARCHITECTS	1,227 FT.	REINFORCED CONCRETE, ALUMINUM, AND GLASS	1992

214 ■ The façade of Central Plaza's tower stands above Hong Kong's forest of skyscrapers. It has a curtain-wall of reflecting glass in various colors, with horizontal bands at the sides and a dark surface with long vertical windows in the center.

215 ■ The atrium is equipped with sculptural escalators and features a rich, oriental taste in its materials and decorations. A pillar in the atrium has been cleverly disguised within a series of geometrical motifs.

CENTRAL Plaza

The triangular shape was chosen because it gives a high percentage of the offices a view over the port. The structure, positioned on the sides and in the center so as to leave a greater area free for the offices, has to deal with problems of static loads that a building of this height incurs as well as strain created by the wind (Hong Kong lies in a region subject to typhoons). For this reason, the engineer Ove Arup originally suggested a steel structure composed of a large outer tube strengthened against the wind with diagonal trusses and a steel core. However, for cost purposes, a similar structure was created in reinforced concrete, which made it necessary to reduce the building's height and increase the size of the base.

The curtain-wall is made of reflecting glass typical in various colors that, alternating with horizontal bands, produce designs on the sides. A dark background with long vertical windows that is illuminated at night with colored neon lights, making the building immediately visible and recognizable, distinguishes the central section. Inside the furnishings are also colorful, shiny, glamorous, and lavish, with details in metal and stone recalling the heyday of New York skyscrapers.

Central PLAZA

216-217 ■ Central Plaza is immediately recognizable in the city because of its height and illumination: after dusk, the vertical windows on the façade are lit up with colored neon lights to emphasize the building's outline.

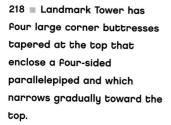

Landmark Tower

At 971 feet, Yokohama's Landmark Tower is the tallest building in Japan, and with its solid but futuristic appearance, it is both a landmark in the city and a symbolic entrance to the country. Its name is derived from the visual role that isolated skyscrapers of extreme height assume in the context of the contemporary metropolis, functioning as oversized icons of the region. The building is the result of an ambition of Otokazu Nakada, the honorary president of Mitsubishi and a former owner of Rockefeller Center, who saw Yokohama razed to the ground at the end of the Second World War. Before his death, he wanted to see the city flourish once more through projects like the Landmark Tower.

Nakada's skyscraper was part of a much wider plan conceived by the city government called Minato Mirai 21, "City-Port of the Twenty-First Century," in which the Nishiku port zone was greatly enlarged both on the existing land and on that recovered from the sea. The aim was to create property speculation that would bring new development to the area and city in general. Landmark Tower was built at the entrance to the new port zone as an intermediary between the ocean and city, and as a symbol of Japan's economic growth.

The building features 52 stories of offices, a 600-bed hotel, a restaurant, and a garden that affords a splendid view of both the Pacific Ocean and Mount Fuji. At street level, Hugh Stubbins

218 ■ Landmark Tower has four large corner buttresses tapered at the top that enclose a four-sided parallelepiped and which narrows gradually toward the top.

219 ■ At 971 feet, the tower is the tallest building in Japan excepting television towers. A feature of the skyline of Japan's second city, it stands beside the Pacific Ocean and is overlooked by Mount Fuji.

Location	Project	Height	Materials	Completion date
Yokohama (Japan)	The Stubbins Associates	971 ft.	Reinforced concrete, steel, and granite	1993

220 left ■ Completely destroyed in the Second World War, the city of Yokohama today has a modern look, with many skyscrapers.

220-221 ■ The façade is composed of alternating bands of glass and granite. As the stone projects further than the glass, the building is given an appearance of solidity and strength.

221 in bottom ■ Landmark Tower is part of a much wider plan to expand the Nishiku port area. The port is the heart of Japan's second-most important city and is its link to the ocean.

(the architect of the Citicorp Center) created a link with the city by means of a five-story public atrium with shops and restaurants. By taking the world's fastest lift from the atrium, it is possible to reach the terrace at the top of the tower in just 40 seconds. Although it was designed by American architects – like many other Asian skyscrapers – a remarkable amount of attention was paid to forms from Japanese tradition and culture such as the comb, the paper lantern, and stacked wood. These distinctive and evocative features charmingly characterize the exterior of the tower, whose forms recall the seventeenth-century Azekura-style Todaiji Temple in Nara.

The building is composed of four large corner buttresses tapered at the top that enclose a four-sided parallelepiped; this recedes gradually toward the top to emphasize the empty space in the center and the use of the corner-based design. Structurally, the tower is formed by a large steel tubular truss plus four steel pylon-type ribs filled with concrete. The structure is completed by a mechanism that reduces the vibrations caused by the wind or potential earthquakes. Emanating a sense of solidity, alternating horizontal bands of glass and granite form the façade.

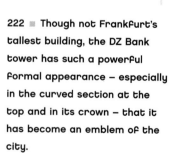

DZ Bank

he Deutsche Zentral-Genossenschaftsbank stands close to the center of Frankfurt, near the central railway station, in an area between the residential district of Westend and the commercial district, on a site adjacent to the Mainzer Landstrasse. The complexity of this area of the city determined the basic rules of this project. Set on the boundary of two urban neighborhoods of different natures, the construction had to be a composition of various volumes with different functions that have multiple relationships with the sections of the districts surrounding it, instead of a single slab of a building like more traditional skyscrapers.

The complex spreads out to encompass a large basilica-like atrium with a transparent, upside-down barrel vault prospectively accentuated by a cantilever roof, a lower L-shaped body, and a higher one consisting of two volumes, the first of which, curved and is topped by a crown, envelops the second one, which is a simple parallelepiped containing the vertical distribution equipment. Whereas the lower body communicates with the residential district as it contains housing and car parking and creates a gradual change of scale between the tower and the city, the higher volume contains the bank's offices and

222 ■ Though not Frankfurt's tallest building, the DZ Bank tower has such a powerful formal appearance — especially in the curved section at the top and in its crown — that it has become an emblem of the city.

223 ■ The diversification of the forms and materials in the volumes was a deliberate choice made by the architect to integrate the building more successfully in its location situated between a residential district and commercial zone.

thus maintains a relationship with the commercial district. The differentiation between the elements is also emphasized by their structure and materials. The structure of the tower consists of dual steel tubes, of which the inner one absorbs the loads while the outer one supports the façade. The lower building is composed of a simple framework structure lined with granite that, thanks to its more traditional look, creates a link with the surrounding buildings. The façade of the curved tower, on the other hand, communicates with the business district, and as such had to have a

more modern and efficient image in order to properly belong to the skyscraper category. The façade, created using a curtainwall of glass and aluminum, gives the building a pure, sculptural-object look.

At 682 feet high, the DZ Bank building has become part of the Frankfurt skyline along with Murphy and Jahn's Messeturm (843 feet) and Foster's Commerzbank (850 feet). Characterizing the downtown area, these three isolated buildings look down on the city like bizarre and slightly shocked giants, symbols of the financial supremacy of this part of Germany.

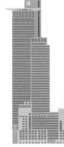

Location	Project	Height	Materials	Completion date
Frankfurt (Germany)	Kohn Pedersen Fox Associates	682 ft.	Concrete, steel, glass, granite, and marble	1993

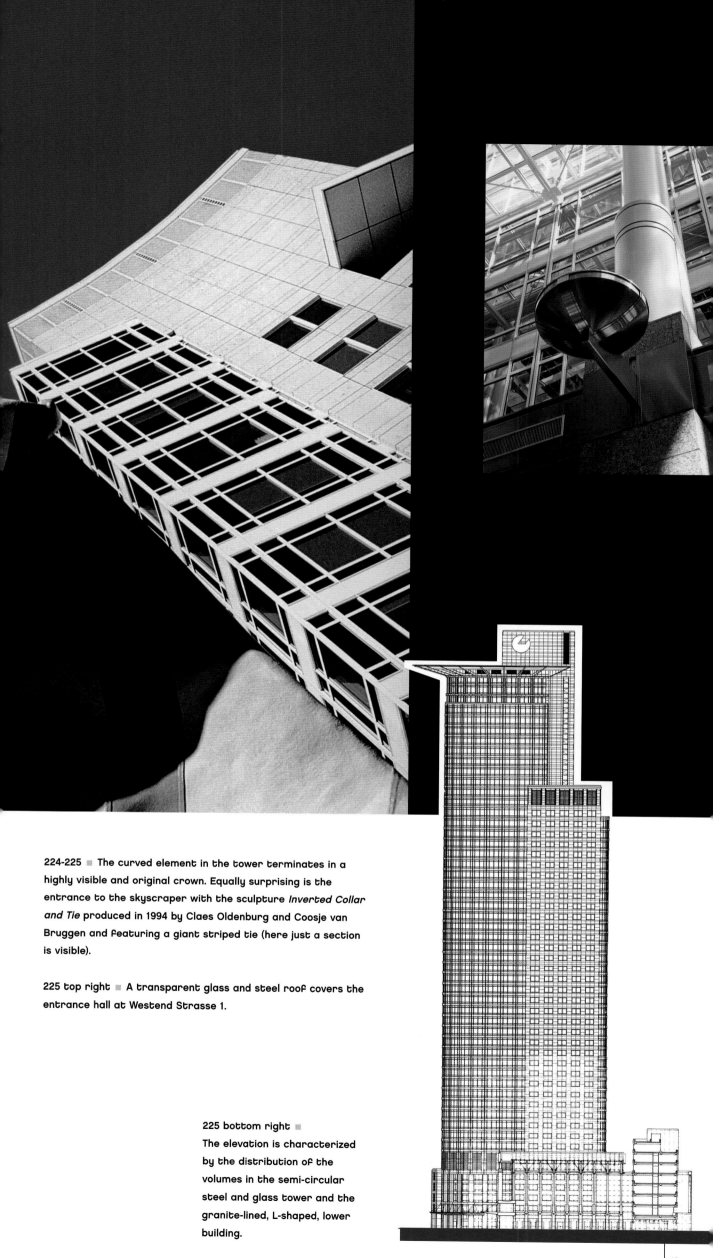

224-225 ■ The curved element in the tower terminates in a highly visible and original crown. Equally surprising is the entrance to the skyscraper with the sculpture *Inverted Collar and Tie* produced in 1994 by Claes Oldenburg and Coosje van Bruggen and featuring a giant striped tie (here just a section is visible).

225 top right ■ A transparent glass and steel roof covers the entrance hall at Westend Strasse 1.

225 bottom right ■ The elevation is characterized by the distribution of the volumes in the semi-circular steel and glass tower and the granite-lined, L-shaped, lower building.

226 ■ The entrance hall to the skyscraper lies between the two taller buildings; its unique, upturned barrel vault can also be seen from outside.

227 top ■ Seen from inside, the upturned barrel vault over the entrance hall creates the illusion of a large steel and glass tent.

Enclosed between these two taller buildings, the DZ Bank is stands out thanks to its crown, which can be seen from around town and, in particular, which recalls the forms of the city's cathedral.

The relationship with the surrounding area is established through a large urban space that lies symmetrically between the two volumes. It includes the entrance hall to the offices, a shopping gallery, restaurants, cafés, and a covered garden that runs north-south so as to receive as much sunlight as possible. Even the façade of the building, formed by a double wall and triple-glazed windows, conserves energy, due to the need to meet the German government's strict environmental regulations.

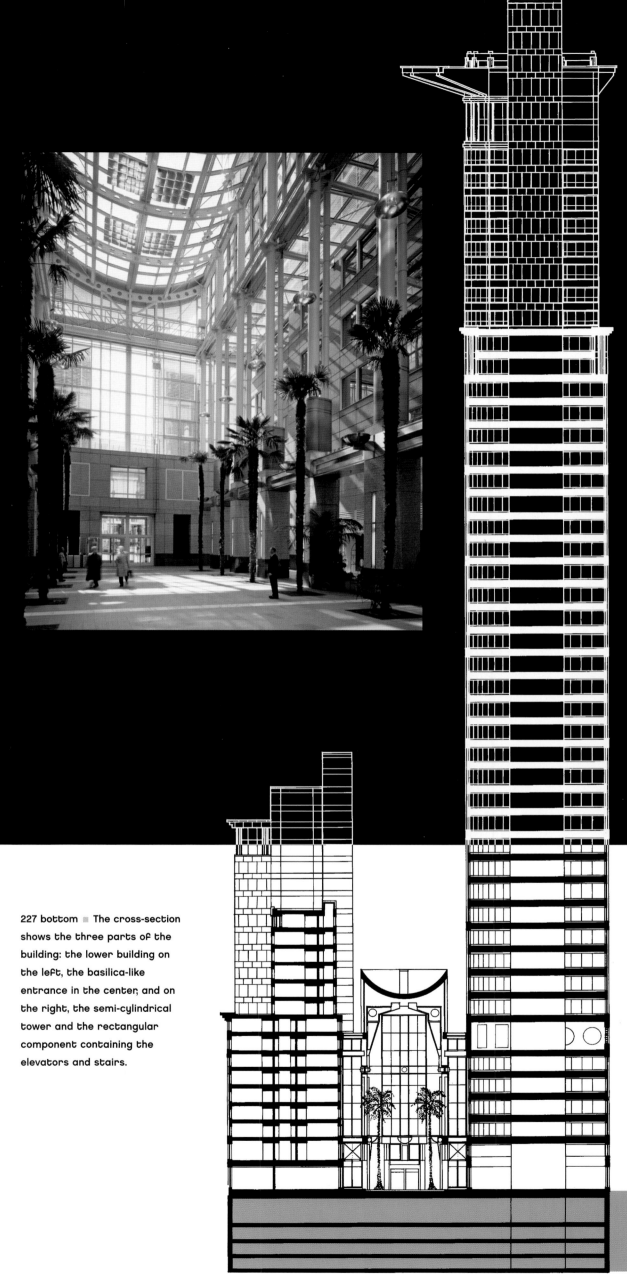

227 bottom ■ The cross-section shows the three parts of the building: the lower building on the left, the basilica-like entrance in the center, and on the right, the semi-cylindrical tower and the rectangular component containing the elevators and stairs.

Citic Plaza

Citic Plaza in Guangzhou (Canton), was Asia's tallest building until 1998 when the Petronas Towers were completed in Kuala Lumpur and the Jin Mao building in Shanghai, however, it remains the tallest building in the world built in reinforced concrete. Citic Plaza is situated on a square lot surrounded by four roads, in an area of great importance in the center of Tianhe commercial district, between the stadium to the north and the railway station to the south (both landmarks take their name from that of the district).

The Plaza has a symmetrical plan that begins with the form of the lot itself, and then rises through a complicated series of intersecting geometrical shapes (a circle inscribed in a square, its diagonals, and two orthogonal axes arranged so that the longer of the two has more importance) that generates further volumes. The complex comprises three buildings including the main tower with 80 stories accommodating offices (except for the lower floors where there are public spaces and shops) and twin 38-story apartment buildings that stand at the sides of the tower. The three different sections are joined by a base containing a 904-space parking lot. The main element is the tower. It has a square plan but is divided into three vertical sections by the differentiation in height of the corner pillars and the central segment. The division is created by both the fact that the

228 ■ The base of the skyscraper is formed by a large portal that contains the cylindrical body of the glass atrium from which projects a cantilever roof. The tower rises above the base.

229 ■ The high-tech appearance of the atrium is created with the use of materials such as glass and steel.

230 top ■ The interiors are decorated elegantly in a blend of modern and Art-Deco styles.

230 bottom ■ A cantilever roof made from steel and glass projects out from the cylindrical body containing the atrium and supporting the tower.

Citic Plaza

231 right ■ The tower is comprised of three parts: these are created by the taller corner pillars, by the differentiated panels on the façade, and by the two low bodies at its base. The result is a highly technological form that stands out in the Guangzhou skyline, making the skyscraper a symbol of the city.

231 left ■ The plans shows the complex's symmetrical plan, which is based on the square shape of the lot and the complicated series of intersections of geometrical figures including a circle, the square of the tower, and the two wings of the lower buildings. It is bordered by four roads: City Road (A), Linhe Dong Lu (Linhe East, B), Tianhe Bei Lu (Tianhe North, C), and Linhe Xi Lu (Linhe West, D).

pillars rise higher and the play of light produced by the panels lining the façade. Although it is 1,283 feet high, the structure of the tower is built of reinforced concrete. It consists of a central core containing the facilities, elevators, and stairs and a row of pillars that ring the perimeter of the building. At the base, the atrium giving access to the offices is composed of a glass cylinder emphasized by a grandiose portal on the outside. The two lower residential buildings are also connected at the base by a concrete and glass cylinder.

Lined completely by high-tech reflecting glass panels, the pure form of the tower gives the building a futuristic image that, with the two spars at the top of the building, characterizes its skyline, of which it has now become a symbol of the city. Overall, the group of buildings has a bizarre appearance that resembles a Chinese mask, especially in its layout.

Location	Project	Height	Materials	Completion date
Guangzhou (China)	Dennis Lau & N.G. Chun Man Architects	1,283 ft.	Reinforced concrete, aluminum, and glass	1997

Commerzbank

T he new headquarters of Commerzbank is the tallest building in Europe at 850 feet, counting the television antennas. The product of the economic expansion that Frankfurt has experienced over recent years, it has become an indispensable reference point on its skyline. This building has brought Norman Foster renown for his skyscraper designs, despite his previous experience with the Hong Kong and Shanghai Bank (1985), in which he began to place greater emphasis on the habitableness of a building and the environmental well-being of its users. It is no accident that Foster's design won the international competition announced in 1991, having gained the support of the Green Party (Germany is the most ecologically minded country in Europe) and of the public. With careful consideration of pollution reduction and problems of scale created by the insertion of such a large building in the city center, the design team worked in close collaboration with the clients, local authorities, and the public in order to immediately create a positive relationship between the city and the skyscraper.

Situated in the heart of Frankfurt and clearly visible from the River Main, it stands between the Kaiserplatz in the city center and the Grosse Gallusstrasse, a very busy road.

232 ■ The exterior of the building clearly shows the structure formed by the three large corner pylons that support the adjoining eight-story office blocks.

233 ■ Using large ropes, two acrobats hoist themselves along the façade of Norman Foster's famous skyscraper in Frankfurt.

Location	Project	Height	Materials	Completion date
FRANKFURT (GERMANY)	NORMAN FOSTER & PARTNERS	850 FT.	REINFORCED CONCRETE, STEEL, AND GLASS	1997

The building is set back from the road and, to express its association with the area, a vast public space was created at the base of the tower surrounded by houses, shops, art galleries, and restaurants. The space is concluded by a large flight of steps leading down to the Grosse Gallusstrasse where the main entrance is and from where the tower can be seen in its entirety. On the Kaiserplatz side, continuity with previously existing buildings was established with a few buildings of the same height to ensure a relationship of scale with the rest of the neighborhood.

Commerzbank's old headquarters, a simple office building esthetically not in

234 top ■ Three-dimensional computer models show the various stages of the skyscraper Foster designed for the bank's Frankfurt headquarters.

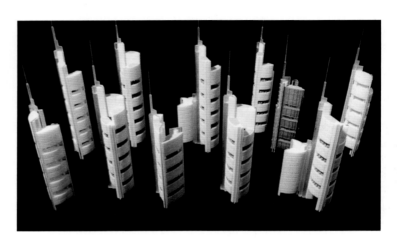

234 bottom ■ The drawings show cross-sections of the Commerzbank's new headquarters. It consists of alternating blocks and empty spaces, with staggered hanging gardens that contribute to the creation of rising air currents. The strategy creates a particular microclimate inside the building.

235 ■ The Commerzbank shares the skyline with many skyscrapers. Frankfurt is one of the few European cities to have allowed high-rise buildings in its center. Besides Foster's building, there are also the Messeturm, Europaturm, and the DZ Bank.

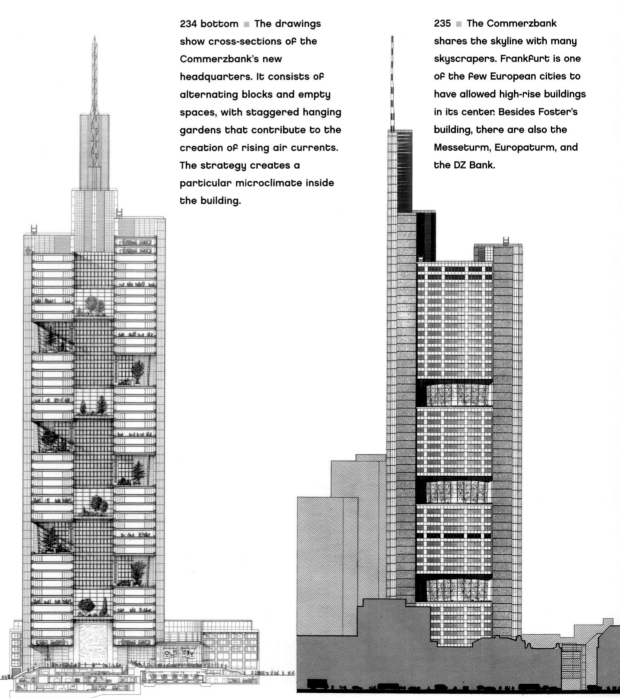

236 ■ The internal façade is a *Klimafassade* formed by a glass panel laminated on the exterior, an air chamber, and a panel that can be opened on the inside to allow for the cooling of the internal air.

237 top ■ The triangular space on the ground floor inside the building is a high atrium covered by a large transparent roof. The view upward inside the atrium is spectacular.

237 center left ■ This view shows one of the hanging gardens. Each one is four stories high.

237 center right ■ Construction of the building shows the three large pylons at the corners of the triangular structure. These support the entire weight of the building and contain the elevators and stairs.

line with the ambitious new project, was also incorporated into the lot. In addition to being a place in which to "live," the new building tries to create an urban space by providing a variety of services to local residents. Apart from its successful insertion into the fabric of the city, the skyscraper won the competition thanks to its bio-climatic and ecologically sustainable qualities provided by some interesting innovations. As Peter Buchanan said, "Foster's eco-tower turns the conventional skyscraper inside out, exposing it to natural light, fresh air, and abundant vegetation, which are found throughout the building."

Completely innovative compared to the traditional view of a skyscraper as a glass box with an internal structural system, the Commerzbank building rests on a structure in which three massive piers stand at the corners of a triangle and contain the elevators

237 bottom ■ The plan shows one of the floors. Given the limited width of the body of the building (49 feet), the offices enjoy natural light and views toward the gardens inside and outward over the city.

238 top ■ The spacious light-filled ground floor offers many recreational areas.

238 bottom ■ Entry to the skyscraper is through a technological sail-shaped covering.

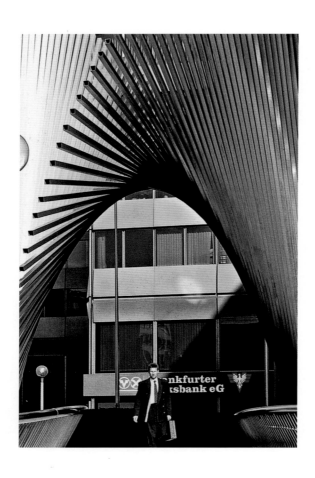

and stairwells. On these, eight floors of offices are attached, thus achieving a span of 49 feet thanks to the use of Vierendeel trusses. The section is formed by alternating blocks and empty spaces, with hanging gardens staggered to form a spiral, which, together with the central shaft of space created by the structural elements being placed at the ends of the building, allow ascending currents of air to be produced. Given the restricted width of the body of the building (49 feet), the offices enjoy natural light and views both internally onto the gardens and externally onto the city. The use of natural light and ventilation brings notable energy savings and a reduction in

238-239 ■ The use of glass and steel gives the bar a high-tech appearance.

239 bottom ■ The cross-section shows the alternation between the eight-story office blocks and the staggered internal hanging gardens, each four stories high.

240-241 ■ At 850 feet tall, the Commerzbank building is currently the tallest building in Europe, not including non-residential structures like television towers. It has become a landmark in the Frankfurt skyline.

sources of pollution. Natural ventilation is created partly by the design of the section, and partly by the use of the *KlimaFassade*, a double façade consisting of a glass panel laminated on the outside, an air chamber, and a panel that opens inward to allow for cooling of the air. In this manner, the façade follows the rules of a new esthetic and is no longer conditioned by the resolution of structural problems but by the environment. It is formed by large empty spaces corresponding to hanging gardens that break up its volume and allow the internal spiral to be

242 ■ The German artist Thomas Emde succeeded in making the most of the structure's nighttime appearance by giving it extraordinary lighting systems. In the evening, the indirect lighting colors the gardens with soft hues while spotlights highlight the upper parts of the façade, accentuating the building's verticality and transforming Frankfurt's skyline.

243 ■ At night, the artful lighting system draws attention to the hanging gardens and office blocks.

observed from the outside. This is a similar solution to that devised by Foster in his designs for the futuristic Millennium Tower, a 2,822-foot-tall pyramid-shaped skyscraper that is supposed to be erected in Tokyo at the end of the first decade of this century.

Foster's eco-compatible experimentation is an integral part of his design for the Swiss Re Tower in London. It is important, however, to emphasize that this type of study began with SOM's design for the National Commercial Bank in Jeddah (1983), the Hong Kong and Shanghai Bank also by Foster (1985), and above all in bio-climatic skyscrapers by Ken Yeang, such as his famous Menara Mesiniaga (1992).

Commerzbank

Petronas Towers

When Sean Connery, the former James Bond, and Catherine Zeta-Jones, one of the most beautiful actresses of the American cinema, dangerously dangle between the Petronas Towers and the walkway that joins them in a dramatic scene from the movie *Entrapment* (about the "theft of the millennium"), the thrills provided by the action inevitably call to mind similar scenes. What was surprisingly new about this film scene was that the setting was not New York and the towers not those of the World Trade Center. Even Hollywood was prepared to recognize the passage of an era, at the end of the second millennium, in the history of city development and architecture.

Starring in this extraordinary symbolic transition in the collective consciousness are the Petronas Towers, the twin towers built at the end of the 1990s in Kuala Lumpur, the capital of Malaysia. Many commentators have noted how the symbolism of the skyscraper belongs explicitly to the joint spheres of political and economic power, and, in this sense, the action scenes filmed in Kuala Lumpur represent a historical shift in importance from the Atlantic to the Pacific. What was only the exotic and distant Far East just a few decades ago has become the "Not Too Far East," as it was brilliantly encapsulated in the title of a recent photography exhibition dedicated to

244 ▪ Constructed in 1998, the Petronas Towers took the record for the world's tallest building from the Sears Tower in Chicago, shifting it for the first time from the Atlantic to the Pacific. Like many Asian skyscrapers, the towers have a bizarre design, which in this case resemble a pagoda.

245 ▪ Standing so tall in the center Kuala Lumpur and typically Malaysian in style, the Petronas Towers have become the symbol of the city and its economic and demographic growth.

the extravagant forms of Asiatic high-rise buildings.

When the first steel and glass skyscrapers were built in Chicago, Kuala Lumpur was at the start of its life as a large, modern city. In 1857, a group of miners founded the city at the confluence of the rivers Klang and Gombak, in a region only partly drained and freed from the dangers of malaria. In 1896, the British governor in Malaysia, who had chosen Kuala Lumpur as his administrative center, planned the rebirth of the city with the construction of a series of brick buildings. It was later chosen as the country's capital by the sultans of the four federated states of Malaysia, who supported its development as a colonial city. When the colonial epoch ended, the history of the country nudged the city in the direction of modernization. In 1974, when it was clear that independent Malaysia had to aim for economic progress and the integration of its three different ethnic groups, Kuala Lumpur was made into a Federal Territory. Even as the World Trade Center and the Sears Tower vied for

Location	Project	Height	Materials	Completion date
Kuala Lumpur (Malaysia)	Cesar Pelli & Associates	1,483 ft.	Concrete, steel, and glass	1998

246 top ■ In every project, the American architect Cesar Pelli combines advanced technology with historical and traditional icons of the local culture. This philosophy won him the competition held in the 1997.

246 bottom and 247 ■ Using an Impressionist-like style, Pelli produced sketches of the projected Petronas Towers using wax pastels that showed the colors and shades altering at different times of the day.

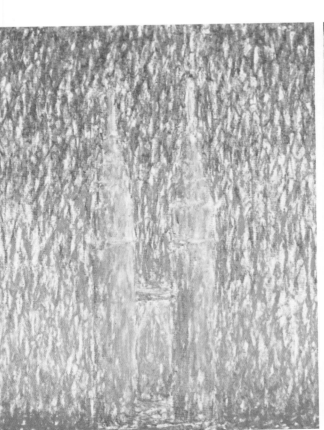

248 and 249 top right ■ Photographs taken during construction show how the towers are made of a reinforced-concrete structure in which the external pillars and core serve as the load-bearing elements. The latter contains the vertical distribution elements and provides anchorage for the floors to give the structure rigidity.

Petronas

249 top lef ■ The model shows the linear appearance of the towers. The inspiration for them was based on two Islamic architectural features: the minaret and the city portal.

249 bottom ■ The top section of the two towers features a faceted spire created by a series of gradual setbacks in the shaft. It culminates in the sphere on which the antenna stands and brings to mind a sort of gateway to heaven. The reflections and shininess of the various materials are fundamental to the design.

supremacy in the United States, Kuala Lumpur was undergoing extraordinary demographic and urban growth.

In 1997, the year in which governmental and municipal powers converged with capitalist interests, a competition was announced for the construction of two towers in the center of the city. The work had to be strongly Malaysian in spirit so that it would become the symbol of the city. The city's central district was chosen where there is a large park, a large variety of other high towers, and a widely spread-out, multi-functional series of buildings that feature architecture based on the traditional Eclectic town houses. The plans that won the competition offered the greatest degree of modern technology and the most extravagant use of historic and traditional local icons. The plan for the Petronas Towers com-

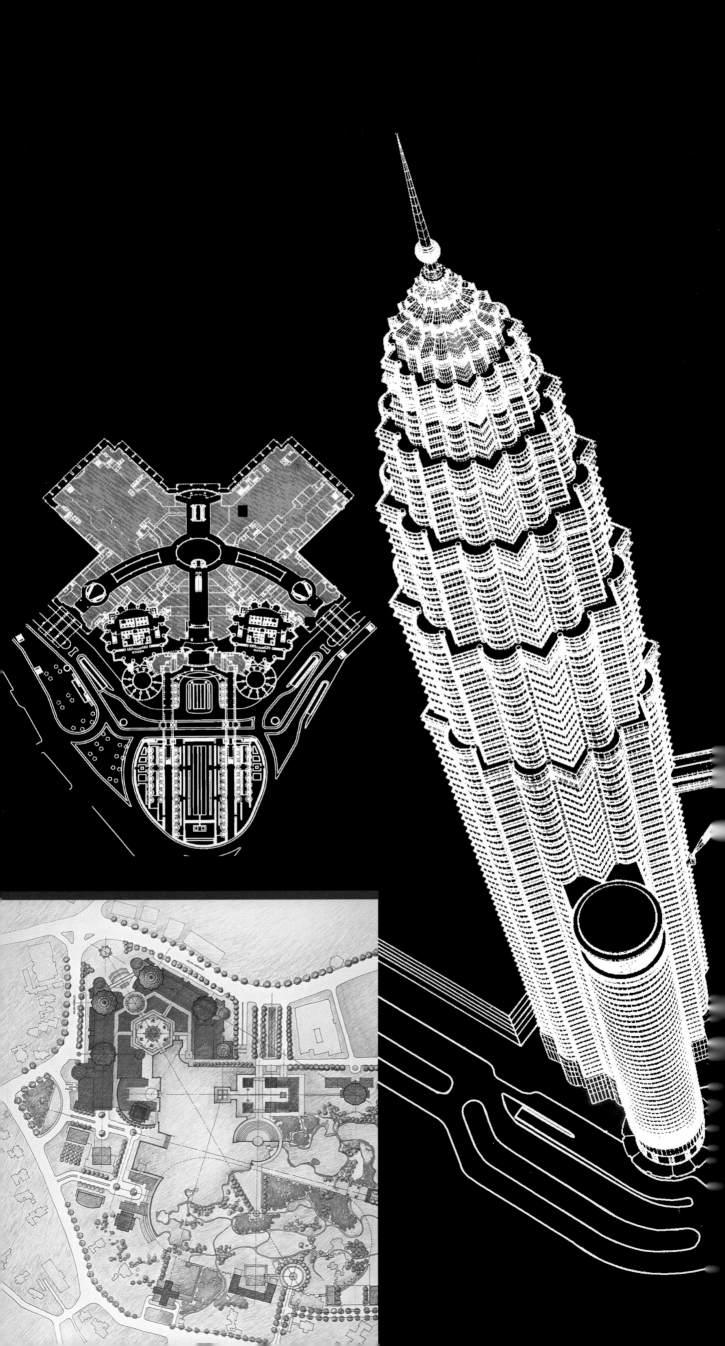

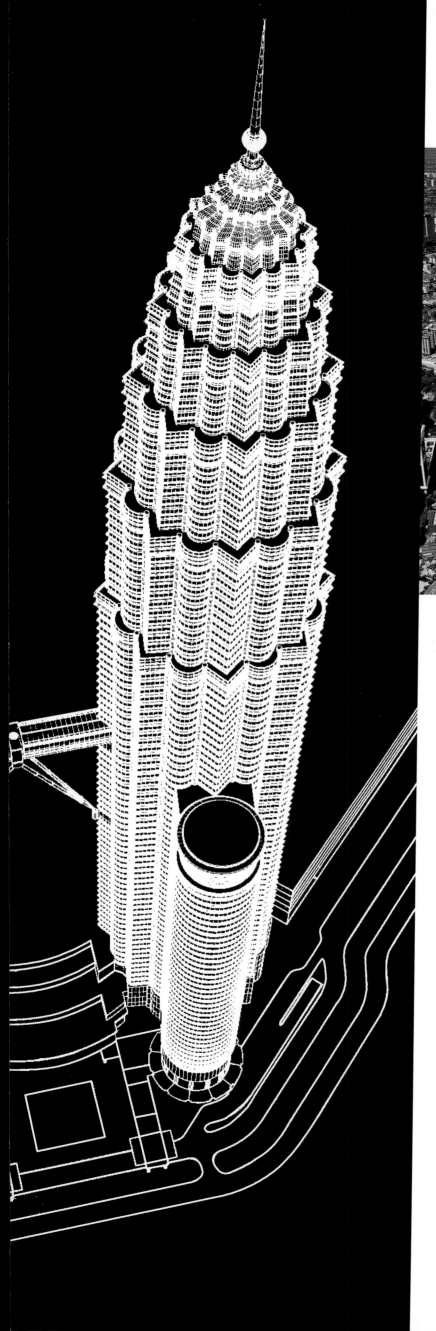

250 top left ■
As shown by the plans, the two towers are connected at the base by a series of low buildings representing interconnected geometric figures. They stand symmetrically on either side of a central axis around which the whole is constructed.

250 bottom left ■
The map shows how the two towers and the buildings at the base are accessed by the large park located in the center of Kuala Lumpur, thus forming the characteristic shape of a portal.

250-251 ■ An axonometric view shows how the form of the towers grows out of a figure in the plan that intersects two squares to become an eight-pointed star.

251 right ■ The Petronas Towers are based on a highly faceted, polylobate cylinder. At a certain point a series of truncated cones emerge, one rising from the other.

Petronas

bined in a single building the greatest height (exceeding the Sears Tower in Chicago), the concept of duality (in the twin towers), the oriental or Islamic use of the symmetrical geometry of squares and circles, and the application of numbers considered to have magical properties. Duality became a building typology and symbolic figure with the construction of the Twin Towers in the World Trade Center in New York, but here it is given a radically different interpretation. Whereas the Twin Towers stood physically separated but closest at their corners like two pure monoliths, the Petronas Towers stand symmetrically opposed, identical, as though reflected at the two sides of an entrance axis with its center at an ambiguous point lying outside the composition. Another feature in Kuala Lumpur is the uninhibited use of a post-modern vocabulary and finely sculpted forms that are typical of

A

B

252 and 253 left ■ The Petronas Towers have been called "technological pagodas." This definition derives from their finely carved forms, oriental design, and the use of advanced instruments, materials, and theories.

253 right ■ The towers are created out of the intersection of two squares, one revolved by 45 degrees with respect to the other. The squares are connected by arches, and pillars stand where the two figures overlap (A). The central structure is characterized by an alternation of two geometrical figures: squares, in the lower section of the towers (B), and circles in the upper section.

255 ■ The façades are lined in glass, aluminum, and stainless steel. Thanks to a mysterious alchemy, the highly technological combination of these materials manages to create decorative effects very similar to those typical of traditional Asian architecture.

Petronas Towers

oriental architectural history. The two buildings resemble minarets where they rise above the pagoda-style portal that represents the entrance to the park, the central district, the capital city, and a hypothetical "gate to heaven."

The form of the towers is given by the growth in height of a figure in the layout that intersects two squares and becomes an eight-pointed star. The result is two polylobate cylinders with many facets from which, at a certain height, rise successive trunks of cone that are slotted telescopically into one another. These culminate in a spire-cum-antenna that points high enough to reach the symbolic and spiritual status of the tallest building in the world, like the winner in some kind of sport competition. Because the chiaroscuro and highlights created by the surfaces are of major importance, the towers are lined with typically oriental decorations made from strongly reflecting materials. The skin of the

254 top ■ The two towers seen from below shoot up toward the sky. At 558 feet, they are joined by a walkway at the 41st and 42nd floors that allows movement between the two.

254 bottom ■ The "skin" on the façade was designed to be ecologically compatible with the demands made on it by the tropical climate and to reflect an authentically Malaysian spirit.

façade meets requirements of ecological compatibility (made necessary by the tropical climate) through several layers and devices, including materials to control lighting and ventilation with control equipment that create strong pictorial effects on the thin, overlapping horizontal bands. This approach and its aesthetic effects are radically different to the traditional and elementary curtain-walls made of metal and glass panels that were typical of International Style. In Kuala Lumpur, the architect Cesar Pelli has succeeded in refining the same esthetic strategy he has adopted in other designs, using materials traditional to non-Western cultures. Thus,

the bizarre Petronas Towers have become emblematic of a dynamic of globalization, which, instead of imposing international hi-tech models on scientifically backward local cultures, have recreated indigenous icons using new technologies. The towers therefore represent to Westerners an urgent invitation to raise their eyes from the commonplace cities of the northern hemisphere, to stop viewing Eastern cultures as exotic, and to recognize the real transformations that the East has contributed to contemporary history.

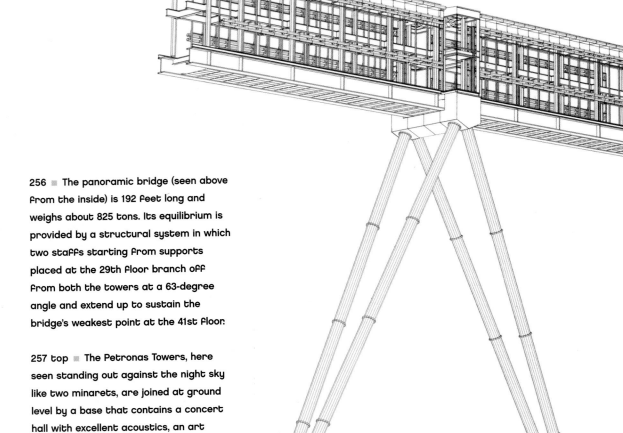

256 ■ The panoramic bridge (seen above from the inside) is 192 feet long and weighs about 825 tons. Its equilibrium is provided by a structural system in which two staffs starting from supports placed at the 29th floor branch off from both the towers at a 63-degree angle and extend up to sustain the bridge's weakest point at the 41st floor.

257 top ■ The Petronas Towers, here seen standing out against the night sky like two minarets, are joined at ground level by a base that contains a concert hall with excellent acoustics, an art gallery, and other structures.

257 bottom ■ The bridge is an essential component of the building in a practical sense since it functions as a link between the two towers, facilitating movement within the complex.

258-259 ■ The top of the towers is formed by a large empty area onto which the floors face. It encloses another cylindrical volume containing the elevators and stairs.

Jin Mao Tower

Jin Mao Tower

"The skyscraper goes East," declared Martin Pawley in 1997 when the record for the world's tallest building shifted from the land where skyscrapers originated – the United States – to the East. To a certain extent, this event is also emblematic of Asian economies overtaking those of the West. The People's Republic of China in particular aims to demonstrate its rapid development and show the world its desire to become one of its foremost economies through the creation of a new image of progress expressed by the skylines of its cities, in particular, Shanghai. This city was the financial capital of the Far East at the start of the twentieth century but went into decline following the Japanese conquest in 1937 and the taking of power by the Communist regime. Today, it is regaining its previous status as an economic and financial pole and growing enormously in size and importance, becoming a true megalopolis deserving of its own symbols. It now boasts outstanding emblems such as the 21st Century Tower by Murphy & Jahn (1998), the World Financial Center by John Pedersen & Fox (1994), and the Jin Mao designed by Skidmore, Owings, & Merrill (SOM), a leading American architectural firms with time-honored experience in designing skyscrapers (among the most famous the John Hancock Center in Chicago built in 1970).

The Jin Mao was built in the district of Pudong on sandy terrain that is subject to both earthquakes and typhoons. There-

260 ■ The height and grandeur of Jin Mao Tower in the city skyline symbolizes the economic and financial growth of the People's Republic of China and the city of Shanghai in particular.

261 ■ The repeated dovetailing seen in the plan and elevation of the skyscraper create an analogy with the pagoda, linking the building with local tradition.

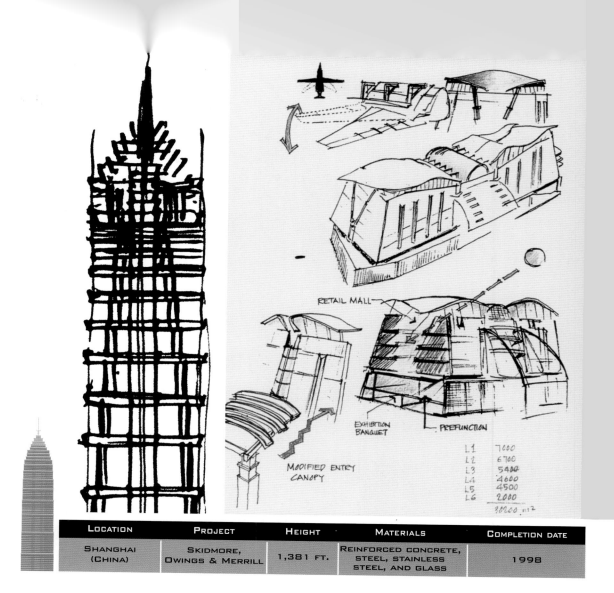

Location	Project	Height	Materials	Completion date
Shanghai (China)	Skidmore, Owings & Merrill	1,381 ft.	Reinforced concrete, steel, stainless steel, and glass	1998

262 ■ The profile of the skyscraper is characterized by the use of technological materials like stainless steel and glass, giving it a futuristic appearance.

263 top ■ These studio sketches show the intention to incorporate the form of the pagoda in the overall design.

fore, the architects chose an avant-garde structure made from a reinforced concrete core and 16 pillars (eight steel and eight concrete) connected by steel trusses. As in Pelli's Petronas Towers, this building incorporates elements that link it to local traditions. With its stepped profile and the crown at the top of the building, it recalls the form of a pagoda, while all its various elements follow the rules of *Fengshui*. This philosophy dictates that the use of the number eight and its multiples bring fortune; hence there are two sets of eight pillars, 88 stories, and so on.

Adrian D. Smith, the member of the SOM team that conceived the building, had prior experience in local architecture and, in this case, he succeeded both in creating an image that has a collective appeal and in integrating the tower in its context. He surrounded it with gardens to create a public area that intermediates between the road and the building.

The design is highly symmetrical. The plan is based on a square with four towers standing on the main axes, where the entrances

263 bottom ■ The glass and steel stairway confirms the intention of the designers to use "technological" materials to declare the modernity of the construction to observers.

264-265 and 264 bottom ■ The interior of the building contains an empty, circular space onto which the floors face and that incorporates the glass tube enclosing the elevators and stairs.

266-267 ■ The eccentric design and 1,381 feet of the Jin Mao Tower have made the building a distinctive feature of the city along with the Radio tower, which exceeds it in height.

are located. Its façade recalls the Bund, an Art Deco district in the Pudong area. It is lined with stainless steel and glass to reflect the changes in light throughout the day, and in the evening, the top of the building is illuminated. With a height of 1,381 feet, the skyscraper is a major reference point in the Shanghai skyline. The first 50 stories are filled with offices, then there are six floors of shops and services, and the final 38 are occupied by a luxury hotel that gives wonderful views across the whole city. From the 56th floor to the top, there is a large empty space at the center that makes the distribution of the hotel components very interesting.

Although Chinese cities are quickly creating symbolic buildings of this kind – partly thanks to the lack of strict building regulations by the Chinese government – local infrastructures are not being improved correspondingly: for the moment heavy traffic and congestion have put a brake on the ambitions of cosmopolitan cities.

Burj Al Arab

The Burj Al Arab is the tallest building with a membrane structure, the tallest hotel in the world, and the only hotel to have been awarded seven stars. It contains an atrium that, at a height of 591 feet, is the highest in the world. This building was designed to break every record and for its construction to be an international event. It appears in modern iconography alongside the Eiffel Tower, the Statue of Liberty, the Sphinx, and London Bridge in a fantastic panorama of the new "wonders of the world." In other words, it is already recognized worldwide. None of its features can pass unobserved, beginning with its sailboat shape. Purposely situated on an artificial island 920 feet from the coast and connected to it by a road, it preserves the privacy of its guests. It is part of the Jumeirah Beach Resort designed by the Scottish architect Jonathan Speirs, who produced this complex as requested by its owner, His Royal Highness Sheikh Mohammed. Inside there are restaurants, gardens, swimming pools, and other buildings, including one that is curved at all levels and therefore referred to as the "wave." The Burj Al Arab has immediately become an icon of the Dubai skyline, which is characterized by a montage of strangely shaped skyscrapers that evoke the sea (with sails and waves), a replica of New York's World Trade Center (the Emirate Twin Towers), and arrangements

268 ■ The sail is the distinctive feature of the Burj Al Arab; a Teflon-lined steel frame made from three enormous pylons, two of which are curved like bows, supports it.

269 ■ The design of the Burj Al Arab was inspired by the sea. It looks like a sail boat docked on an artificial island, which was actually specially built 919 feet from the coast and where its guests can find a truly exclusive atmosphere.

of geometrical prisms cut diagonally according to reinterpretations of Middle Eastern architecture featuring such forms as arches, vaults, domes, and spheres.

Construction of this exceptional building began in 1994 and immediately became a challenge to the most advanced technologies known. Piles were implanted 130 feet into the sea bed, and the construction of the sail required the creation of a steel skeleton formed by three huge piers placed on the vertical axes of a triangular plan, two of which curve like arches to meet the third, straight one at the top. They are connected by horizontal trusses that are further strengthened by diagonal reticular girders. Behind this structure, a shield made of a double skin lined with Teflon protects the building from the heat and light of the desert. Set back from the structure and ending, due to their pointed shape, before the top of the building, the façades

Location	Project	Height	Materials	Completion date
Dubai (United Arab Emirates)	W. S. Atkins & Partners	1,053 ft.	Steel and glass	1999

271 bottom ■ The tower is part of a series of buildings that spread onto the mainland, including one in the original form of a wave.

270-271 ■ Burj Al Arab's isolated position emphasizes the basic concept of the project: a sailboat skyscraper and a hotel serving as a refuge reserved for the privileged few.

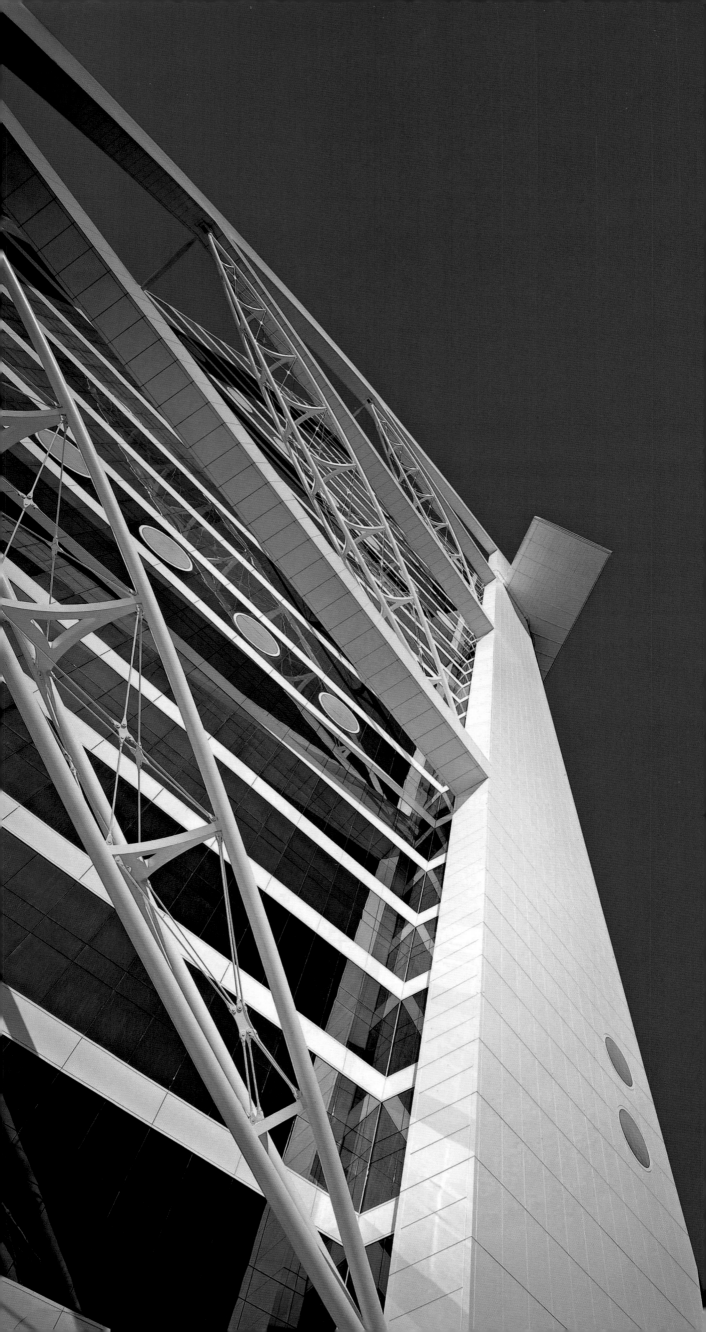

Burj Al Arab

272 ■ The side façade displays the structure made from horizontal and diagonal girders behind which can be discerned the glass- and Teflon-fiber curtain-wall.

273 ■ A round projecting platform at the top of the building is the hotel's helipad.

give the building a highly technological image symbolizing the progress and modernity of the country. No doubt, many other future buildings will use a similar image. The top of the construction is characterized by an empty space where the three piers meet and by an antenna. There is also a circular heliport, set apart from the structure, and a restaurant, which is also suspended in the air 656 feet above sea level and reached by an external express, panoramic elevator. The restaurant gives a marvelous view over the Persian Gulf and the city of Dubai.

Visible and recognizable from afar by day because of its unique form and daz-zling white structure, at night it changes dramatically due to the way in which it is lit up. The use of a wide variety of colors and a large number of spotlights creates a spectacular effect, evoking images that seem to come more from *One Thousand and One Nights* than reality. The interior is also opulent, extravagant, and magnificent thanks to the combination of advanced technologies with local traditional taste in the decorations and furnishings. The constant blend of global and local, old and new, is a contrast typical of modern Dubai. The hotel does not have rooms but two-floor suites, each equipped with portable computers, Internet connections, and

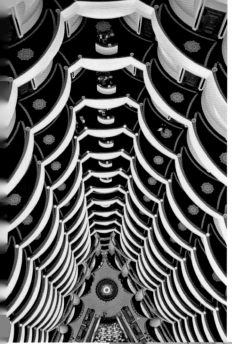

274 ■ The suites face onto a large open space at the center of the building that acts as a 54-floor-high light well.

275 ■ The empty space of the atrium is decorated with a luxurious style with a large staircase, a giant order of tapered columns, and intersecting archways typical of Islamic architecture. The effect is quite spectacular.

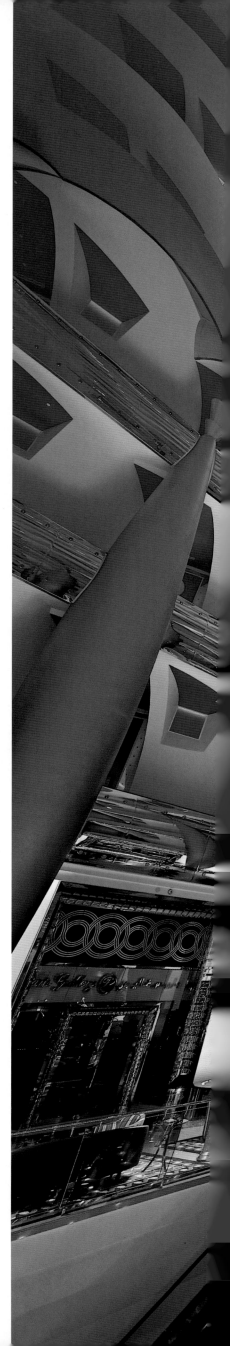

televisions. The royal suite has a revolving bed, an elevator, and a private cinema. At the center of the building, there is a large empty space — a well of light — 54 stories high onto which the suites face. This too is richly decorated and luxurious, perhaps overly so (it has been compared to Las Vegas), and attempts to create a sequence of extraordinary settings through a huge stairway, a colonnade consisting of giant columns tapered both at the top and bottom, and intertwining and overlaid archways that evoke motifs typical of Islamic culture.

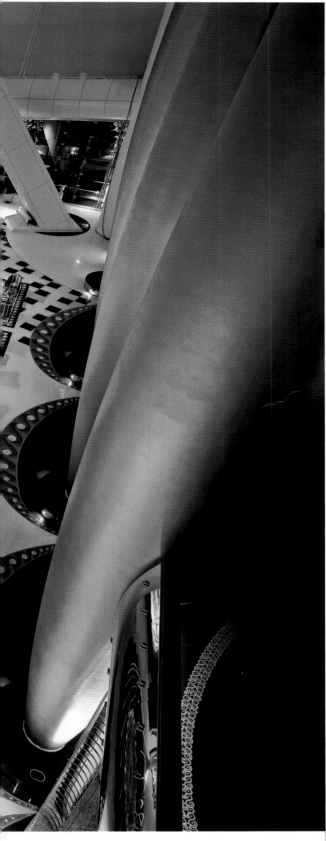

276 bottom ■ The reading room in the Assawan Spa and Health Club recalls the atmosphere of the ancient baths of Middle Eastern countries.

277 top ■ The 202 suites of the hotel all have two floors and are equipped with every amenity from internet connections to plasma-screen televisions.

277 bottom ■ The grand staircase leading to the royal suites, which occupy the entire 25th floor, is only an opulent alternative to the more practical private elevator, just one of the many, extraordinary amenities furnished by the most exclusive part of the hotel. The Royal Suite is actually equipped with an enormous dining room, a meeting space in Arab style, and a private movie theater.

276-277 ■ Mosaic floors and bulging colossal columns welcome guests to the impressive atrium blazing in a golden hue.

278 top ■ The Al Mahara Seafood Restaurant, the hotel's underwater restaurant, is reachable via a short trip aboard a small submarine that departs from the lobby of the Burj Al Arab.

278 center ■ The sitting room of one of the suites reveals a taste for opulent decoration to accompany the services and advanced technology offered.

278 bottom ■ The royal suite has a revolving canopy bed and remarkably rich decoration, with elegant black and gold columns, inlaid tables, and ubiquitous references to Middle Eastern culture.

279 ■ Even the swimming pool of the Assawan Spa and Health Club on the 18th floor is decorated in Islamic style, with columns, colored mosaics, and geometric motifs emphasized by dramatic lighting effects.

Condé Nast Building

T he Condé Nast Building, located between Broadway and 42nd Street, was part of a larger project to renovate 42nd Street and Times Square (which also led to the Reuters Building by Fox and Fowle and E Walk by Arquitectonica). Its construction raised a debate, unusual for the United States but common in Europe, over the character of the city's historic center. During the 1930s and 40s, development in Manhattan was concentrated in Midtown with the construction of superb skyscrapers like the Chrysler and Empire State, and in the 1970s in the Downtown area with the World Trade Center. Since the late 1990s, however, Manhattan has had to evaluate the renovation of its original core. This resulted in the reconstruction of a skyscraper that looks down on Times Square and through which Broadway also passes. For this reason, in 1995 City Hall chose the architectural firm of Fox and Fowle, well known as designers of ecologically sustainable buildings that were highly respectful of their environments. Because the revitalization of the square would inevitably give it a new image, the city and community were naturally concerned about the impact that a 48-story office block would have on the surrounding area. However, the design that the firm pro-

280 ■ The Condé Nast Building is composed of two interlocked parallelepiped buildings: the lower brick-covered one to the east and the one to the west with a glass and steel façade, which also acts as a covering for the lower building.

281 ■ The Condé Nast Building stands in Times Square on the corner of Broadway and 42nd Street. It is part of a larger program to renovate the heart of Manhattan. A fundamental aspect of the project was the new skyscraper's ability to fit harmoniously into its surroundings.

Location	Project	Height	Materials	Completion date
NEW YORK (U.S.A.)	FOX AND FOWLE ARCHITECTS, P. C.	810 FT.	REINFORCED CONCRETE, ALUMINUM, AND GLASS	1999

duced seems to have been satisfactory, and even the *New York Times* has declared that the Condé Nast Building could have been much more out of scale given the towers that have recently been put up on Broadway. The building seems to have been deconstructed and then rebuilt to harmonize with the site.

It has two types of façade: the west side has a curtain-wall made from steel and glass, and the lower section is studded with billboards as is traditional in the pop culture of Times Square. Meanwhile, the east façade is in brick to complement the elegant setting of Bryant Park. The use of sustainable architecture is more evident inside where the use of natural light has been maximized. Energy is produced using photovoltaic cells and a specifically coordinated system to control the temperature that, functioning in tandem with a wastewater system, cools the air and thereby minimizes consumption of polluting fuels. In

282 ■ The top of the building on the Times Square side features a steel and glass curtain-wall.

283 ■ With a glass wall at the top and a brick wall at the bottom, the skyscraper blends harmoniously into the elegant setting of nearby Bryant Park.

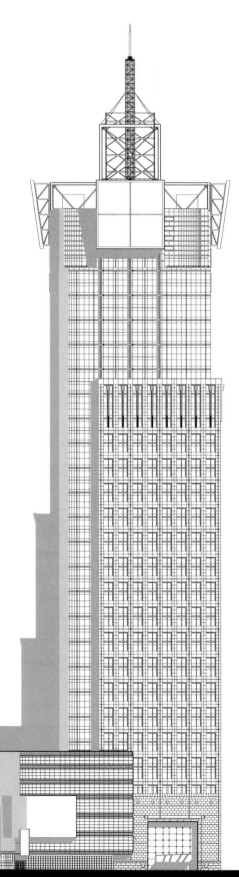

CONDÉ Nast

addition, all the interior decoration was chosen for its recyclable qualities and the sustainability of its materials. A remarkable feature of the building is the café on the 40th floor designed by Frank O. Gehry. It is decorated using blue titanium and a veneer of steel and ash wood. The main eating areas are placed along the perimeter of the building, while curved glass walls enclose the tables in the center, giving the setting an intimate yet open feel.

The Condé Nast Building was built according to the most modern criteria and techniques available. Only two accidents, which occurred during construction, risked tarnishing the nascent image of this new Manhattan landmark. However, these unfortunate events of 1999 did not impede completion of the building. After construction, it received recognition by the National American Institute of Architects and the AIA of the State of New York for its exceptional technological and ecological qualities.

Emirates Twin Towers

Emirates Twin Towers

The height and position of the Emirates Twin Towers on Sheikh Zayed Road make them the backdrop to the central commercial district in Dubai, the second largest city in the United Arab Emirates. The symbol of the enormous development this region is undergoing, these towers with their twin image reflect a recurring architectural feature seen in earlier examples, including the Twin Towers in New York, Marina City in Chicago, the Rialto Towers in Melbourne, and the Petronas Towers in Kuala Lumpur. It is an image that belongs to late-modern Mannerism in which the latest construction technologies are linked to the use of a geometrical figure rendering the building immediately recognizable. In this case, the building's most distinctive feature is the triangle, a figure dear to Islamic art, which is used repeatedly throughout the design. Indeed, the building's plan is in the shape of an equilateral triangle; the glass roofs and skylights are triangular, the covering element is an oblique pyramid, and the internal and external floors are decorated with many examples of triangles.

286 and 287 top ■ The towers are formed by the intersection of a triangular parallelepiped and a cylinder. The two volumes are differentiated by the pattern and degree of transparency of their reflecting glass panels.

287 bottom ■ The top of the tower is very distinctive compared to the rest of the building: it features an oblique pyramid with a triangular lantern below which open vertical windows (instead of horizontal ones as seen in the rest of the structure), a cylinder inserted in a corner, and an big antenna right at the very top.

LOCATION	PROJECT	HEIGHT	MATERIALS	COMPLETION DATE
DUBAI (UNITED ARAB EMIRATES)	NORR GROUP CONSULTANTS INTERNATIONAL	1,165-1,014 FT.	REINFORCED CONCRETE, ALUMINUM, AND GLASS	2000

288 top ■ The project calls for a vast empty space inside the buildings containing the high-tech elevators and stairs and onto which face all the floors. In the lower tower, which accommodates the luxurious 48-story Emirates Towers Hotel, this space is occupied by the lobby.

288-289 ■ A glass elevator rising from the hotel's atrium allows guests to admire the building's structure, built – like its twin – on an equilateral-triangle plan, from within.

The main tower contains offices, meeting rooms, and a business center. In height, it is one of the 20 highest buildings in the world and among the tallest in the Middle East and the entire Mediterranean region. The lower of the two towers has a 400-room luxury hotel, exclusive clubs, meeting rooms, a 9,700-square-foot ballroom, a sports center, and a restaurant on the top floor from which a splendid view over the coast can be admired.

The terraced base is also created out of triangular figures and curves, out of which the two towers rise. It stands on park grounds surrounded by large infrastructures, and contains shops, restaurants, covered parking for 1,800 cars, and an atrium featuring waterfalls that leads to the hotel. The image projected by the base contrasts with that of the towers for the softness of its curves and for its materials: the base is lined with granite whereas the towers are lined with steel, copper, and reflecting glass. Their shiny exterior

289 ■ The Emirates Towers Hotel is the perfect building for executives on business trips. A splendid view of the city can be had from the lounge of the Executive Club (top) whereas the enormous ballroom with its lively floor featuring motifs typical of local art (bottom) often functions as a conference room.

and slender duality make the towers immediately recognizable even from a distance, and they have become a landmark in these arid and monotonous surroundings in which there are no particularly outstanding features. The complex also boasts a square embellished with fountains and steel sculptures.

The success of the design of the Emirates Twin Towers is the result of the successful combination of advanced technology, a futuristic image, and traditional architectural elements of the region.

290 top ■ The interior of the building features sitting rooms, like those of the Presidential Suite, in which businessmen can meet in an environment equipped with all the services necessary to help them in their tasks.

290 bottom ■ The rooms in the hotel (like this one in the Apex Suite) are filled with light, thanks to the large windows.

291 ■ The two towers rise out of a curvy-shaped terraced base set on grounds surrounded by large roads. Thanks to their unique forms, the buildings have become an important landmark in Dubai.

Al Faisaliah Center

The Al Faisaliah Center was of fundamental importance to the development of Riyadh and Saudi Arabia as it was the first skyscraper to be built in the country. Its unusual shape, like a pinnacle piercing the sky, can be seen from every point in the city and has changed the city's skyline. The building has become not only the symbol of Riyadh but also an emblem of a rapidly developing society whose international importance is continuously growing. The British architect to whom the project was entrusted, Norman Foster, commented, "the opportunity to design the first sky-scraper in Riyadh and Saudi Arabia was a tremendous responsibility for me. I wanted it to be not just original but something the community would be proud of in the years to come." Foster certainly succeeded in his intentions.

The Al Faisaliah Center was inaugurated on May 13, 2000, three years after construction commenced, with a large celebration at which the highest authorities in the country were present. It has undoubtedly become an officially recognized symbol for most of the population. Sited in Riyadh's most prestigious residential and commercial district (the buildings in Riyadh are mostly low and horizontal and the city is threaded by wide roads and fast-moving traffic), the complex has been defined "a part of the city within the city." It is a place where

292 ■ The Al Faisaliah Center, in the center of the residential and commercial neighborhoods of the capital of Saudi Arabia, it can be seen from any point in the city. As the first skyscraper to be built in this country, the building marked a fundamental point in Riyadh's development.

293 ■ The uppermost section is empty, with a series of extraordinary elements inside. A three-story-tall orb lined with gilded glass is surmounted by a lantern decorated with steel geometric motifs above which rises a green glass spire.

294 left ■ The skyscraper includes a five-story atrium that connects the north section (containing the hotel) to the south section (where the apartments and shops are located). It is enclosed by walls decorated with colored glass.

294 right ■ The tower has a square plan rotated by 45 degrees relative to the bilateral symmetrical axis. It is preceded by a wide space lined by two rows of palms that symmetrically emphasize the axis, culminating visually in the edge of the skyscraper.

residents can live, work, and enjoy their free time. It contains offices, a five-star hotel, a banquet and conference center, a shopping mall, luxury apartments, and a high-quality restaurant in the orb at the top, offering fantastic views of the city.

The tower is based on a four-sided pyramid (previously seen in skyscrapers such as the Transamerica Pyramid and John Hancock Center) that is lightened by the façades and reinforced at the corners with four angular bow-shaped ribs joined at the top in a spire. Overall, it forms an assembly of explicitly non-western and vaguely fanciful figures. The structure is formed by the central core containing the elevators and stairs, and the four corner ribs. The slenderness of the ribs makes the tower appear extremely slim, and this impression is accentuated by the fact that no particular form is discernible as the light aluminum curtain-wall is recessed and ends before the top of the building. The result is that the uppermost section seems empty, with a series of extraordinary elements inside: a three-story-high orb lined with gilded glass, the lantern decorated with steel "cruciform flowers," and the green glass spire. The base of the tower is a square rotated by 45 degrees from the main site axis and has a five-story atrium that connects the hotel with the apartments and shops. Covered by a roof composed of aluminum "petals," the atrium is lined with large window panels portraying the desert and other natural and environmental features of the country.

Naturally, any work by Norman Foster, especially one located in the desert, contains a heat-resistance system. Here, it is incorporated into the façade in which the aluminum panels move depending on the quantity of light to reflect the glare of the sun and regulate the heat absorbed.

Location	Project	Height	Materials	Completion date
Riyadh (Saudi Arabia)	Norman Foster	876 ft.	Steel and Aluminum	2000

DEBENHAMS

Kingdom

Kingdom Center

The eccentric forms of the Al-Faisaliah Center by Norman Foster, completed in May 2000, and the Kingdom Center by the American architect Ellerbe Becket, completed in January 2001, have radically changed the Riyadh skyline. Before their construction, it was better characterized by extensive and largely horizontal development (in which buildings on average do not exceed five sto-

KINGDOM CENTER

296

Center

296-297 ■ The Kingdom Center's
appearance mutates with the changing
of the lights at the top, reigning
supreme over Riyadh and enlivening the
otherwise horizontal panorama.

ries) and a heavy presence of roads of fast-moving traffic.

Both were built for Prince Al-Walid, the grandson of the kingdom's founder King Abdul Aziz and a great admirer of advanced technologies and modern design. His aim was to realize buildings that would be recognized internationally as symbolic of Riyadh and Saudia Arabia, and which would represent

the growing role of this country in the world economy.

When the international competition for the design of the Kingdom Center was announced, the prince invited roughly one hundred of the world's most famous architectural firms to taken part. It was won by Ellerbe Becket, whose design matched the prince's idea of a simple and powerful struc-

298 top ■ The entrance to the building is a triumph of intersecting forms and rich and shiny materials such as marble, chrome, gilding, and colored glass. A significant feature is the gigantic cantilever roof over the entrance.

298 bottom ■ The tube-shaped skyscraper stands on an oval plan and culminates in a downward parabolic curve.

299 top ■ The interiors are as modern and technological as the exterior. The integrated materials and forms provide a sense of efficiency and essentiality.

299 bottom ■ In addition to the skyscraper, the plans include other lower buildings and recreational grounds, all laid out symmetrically.

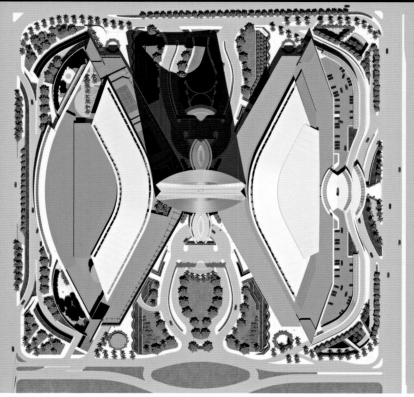

Location	Project	Height	Materials	Completion date
Riyadh (Saudi Arabia)	Ellerbe Becket and Omrania Consortium	971 ft.	Steel, reinforced concrete, glass, granite, and aluminum	2002

ture that would also convey a sense of power and monolithic qualities and be based on a symmetrical plan to express an international rather than local flavor. The winning design features a thin tube rising from an elliptical plan and ends in a lowered parabolic curve. Like all skyscrapers that take inspiration from the world of industrial design in which prevail the forms of common, everyday objects, in the same way that Philip Stark's design for a lemon squeezer looks like an octopus, this building resembles a corkscrew rather than a skyscraper. Its original and highly recognizable form is tied to the fact that Riyadh's construction regulations prescribe a maximum height of 98 feet for new buildings. However, having exceeded this height, to create a building visible from every point, Becket designed a sculptural object, an empty space that is uninhabitable except for the lookout platform on its top, formed by a bridge of 197 feet connecting the two ends of the curve. This makes it Saudi Arabia's highest building.

KINGDOM Center

300 top ■ The interior spaces have complex volumes with high vaults that are looked onto by landings and bridges joining the lower lateral spaces.

300 center ■ The group of buildings serves many public functions, including a large shopping mall.

300 bottom ■ All the interior spaces have pools of water, fountains, and local plants to enhance the sense of lightness created by the materials used.

301 ■ With its futuristic exterior lined with aluminum and reflective glass, the Kingdom Center has become one of the icons of Riyadh and Saudi Arabia. As wished by those who commissioned it, the skyscraper stands as a symbol of the growing role that Saudi Arabia is playing in the world economy.

This skyscraper combines modern esthetics and advanced technology with the traditional customs of the Islamic world. Its external appearance is futuristic thanks to its reflecting glass and aluminum lining, while inside there is the prince's business headquarters, a luxury hotel, a three-floor shopping mall, a conference hall, a banquet hall, offices, a sports club, and apartments. Out of respect to Saudi customs, it also includes prayer halls and an entire floor devoted to a shopping mall for women only. Accessed by a separate entrance, inside women are free not to wear the veil.

Tomorrow Square

Tomorrow Square

302 ■ The roof of the concrete and glass Tomorrow Square has four sloping sides and transparent sections on the axes. At night, these are lit up to create a splendid lantern.

303 ■ The skyscraper's structure is made entirely from reinforced concrete and has a frame visible from the outside. The structure's sturdiness allows the tower to withstand high winds and earthquakes.

Tomorrow Square, the third highest skyscraper in Shanghai, is part of one of the most bizarre skylines in the Far East, which is composed of a motley and extravagant collection of skyscrapers, tall buildings, and TV towers of all shapes and sizes. One of these is the Oriental Pearl, which, at 1,536 feet, is the tallest structure in China though it only has 14 stories situated in two suspended spheres and three observation levels, the highest of which is at 1,148 feet. In such a setting, Tomorrow Square could not but have an extravagant form; it is composed of two parallelepip with a square base attached up to a c tain height, above which the taller of two remains free. Crowned by a roof w four strongly sloping sides and cut on axes by transparent sections, at night turns into a fantastic lantern.

This building was designed by the fam American architect John Portman, inventor of "promotional architecture," which architecture is considered sim another publicity medium. In this case, has again created a dramatic and surp ing design that carries an advertising m

sage. After designing many hotels in the United States, with this project Portman made the switch to Asia in creating a multifunctional skyscraper that would contain offices, residential units (the apartments in the upper part of the tower are the highest in Shanghai), and a hotel. As in all his designs, the building had to be both a part of the city and meet all its inhabitants' needs and requirements.

The engineers who built the skyscraper accepted such an unusual form as a chal-lenge, envisioning a structure made entirely from reinforced concrete with floors composed only of thin slabs for the hotel's floors, and floors with girders for the offices. They designed an external frame so that the tower – being slender for its height – is able to resist both the forces of the wind and earthquakes. Because of the threat of earthquakes, the building has foundations 250 feet deep, which give Tomorrow Square stability despite its remarkable height.

TOMORROW Square

304-305 ■ Tomorrow Square is a distinctive
feature of Shanghai's skyline, one of the most
varied in the world. The Shanghai locality in which
the skyscraper stands is one of the best
organized in the city.

LOCATION	PROJECT	HEIGHT	MATERIALS	COMPLETION DATE
SHANGHAI (CHINA)	JOHN PORTMAN & ASSOCIATES	935 FT.	REINFORCED CONCRETE AND GLASS	2003

INDEX

INDEX

INDEX

INDEX

PHOTO CREDITS

PHOTO CREDITS

PHOTO CREDITS

PHOTO CREDITS

Page 274 **bottom** Jumeirah International
Pages 274-275 Jumeirah International
Pages 276-277 Jumeirah International
Page 276 Jumeirah International
Page 277 **top** Jumeirah International
Page 277 **bottom** Jumeirah International
Page 278 **top** Jumeirah International
Page 278 **center**, Jumeirah International
Page 278 **bottom** Jumeirah International
Page 278-279 Jumeirah International
Page 280 A. Attini/Archivio White Star
Page 281 A. Attini/Archivio White Star
Pages 282-283 A. Attini/Archivio White Star
Page 283 kindly provided by Fox & Fowle Architects
Page 284 **top** kindly provided by Fox & Fowle Architects
Page 284 **bottom** kindly provided by Fox & Fowle Architects
Page 285 kindly provided by Fox & Fowle Architects
Page 286 Artur Photo
Page 287 **top** Jumeirah International
Page 287 **bottom** P. Beckers-Skyscraper Picture Collection
Page 288 **top** Jumeirah International
Pages 288-289 T. Wheeler/LPI
Page 289 **top** Jumeirah International
Page 289 **bottom** Jumeirah International
Page 290 **top** Jumeirah International
Page 290 **bottom** Jumeirah International
Pages 290-291 Jumeirah International
Page 292 J. Poon, kindly provided by Foster and Partners

Page 293 kindly provided by Rosewood Hotels & Resorts
Page 294 **top** J. Poon, kindly provided by Foster and Partners
Page 294 **bottom** kindly provided by Foster and Partners
Page 295 **top** kindly provided by Rosewood Hotels & Resorts
Page 295 **bottom** N. Young, kindly provided by Foster and Partners
Page 296 J. Poon
Page 297 J. Poon
Page 298 **top** J. Poon
Page 298 **bottom** R. Wright, kindly provided by Ellerbe Becket
Page 299 **top** J. Poon
Page 299 **bottom** kindly provided by Ellerbe Becket
Page 300 **top** J. Poon
Page 300 **center**, J. Poon
Page 300 **bottom** J. Poon
Page 301 J. Poon
Page 302 kindly provided by John Portman & Associates
Page 303 kindly provided by John Portman & Associates
Pages 304-305 L. Liqun/Corbis/Contrasto

All the drawings of the skyscrapers are by Archivio White Star

BIBLIOGRAPHY

Eric J. Hobsbawm, *Il secolo breve*, Rizzoli, Milan 1995

Francis Scott Fitzgerald, *L'età del jazz*, Casa editrice Il Saggiatore, Milan 1960

Mario Campi, Skyscrapers. *An architectural Type of Modern Urbanism*, ETH Zurich Department of Architecture, Birkhauser, Basle 2000

Judith Dupré, *Gratte-ciel du monde*, Edition Française, Konemann Verlagsgesellschaft mbHD-58968, Cologne

Mario Panizza, *Mister grattacielo*, Laterza, Roma-Bari, 1990

Rem Koolhaas, *Delirious New York*, Electa, Milan, 2001 (original edit. 1978)

Nik Cohn, *Broadway. Storie dal cuore del mondo*, Einaudi, Turin, 1993

Next.8. 'Mostra Internazionale di Architettura', *La Biennale di Venezia*, Marsilio, Padua, 2002

Jean Baudrillard, Jean Nouvel, *Les objets singuliers. Architecture et philosophie*, Calmann-Lévy, Paris, Editions de la Villette, 2000

Antonino Terranova, *Mostri Metropolitani*, Meltemi editore srl, Rome, 2001

David Bennett, *Grattacieli.Come sono, dove sono, come si costruiscono gli edifici più alti del mondo*, Istituto Geografico De Agostini SPA, Novara, 1996

Rowan Moore, *Vertigo.The strange New World of the contemporary city*, Laurence King Publishing in association with Glasgow, 1999

Warren I. Cohen, *Il secolo del Pacifico. Asia e America al centro del mondo*

NOTSOFAREAST. *Immagini tra Pechino e Shanghai di Olivo Barbieri*, Donzelli Editore, Rome, 2002

ACKNOWLEDGMENTS

The publisher would like to thank the following for their contributions.
Architectural studios:
Foster and Partners
Cesar Pelli & Associates
Skidmore, Owings & Merrill LLP
John Portman & Associates
Zeidler Grinnell Partnership/Architects
Murphy/Jahn Architects
Kohn Pedersen Fox Associates PC
Loebl Schlossman & Hackl
Dennis Lau & Ng Chun Man Architects & Engineers Ltd
Fox & Fowle Architects
Ellerbe Becket

And also:
Amy Bissonette, Ryerson & Burnham Libraries, The Art Institute of Chicago
Jumeirah International
Al Faisaliah Hotel, Rosewood Hotels & Resorts
Institut français d'architecture, Paris
Yokohama Royal Park Hotel
President R. Formigoni, Assessore G. Della Frera and architect R. Todaro of the Regione Lombardia
The Author would like to thank Mrs. Alessandra Criconia for reviewing the introduction and Gianpaola Spirito for editing text and captions.

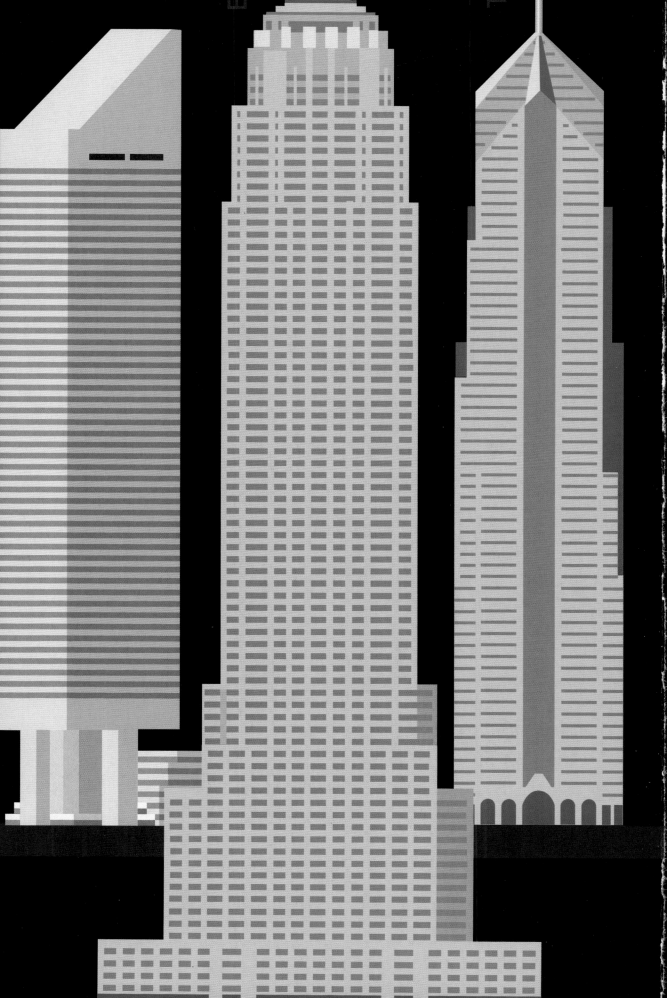

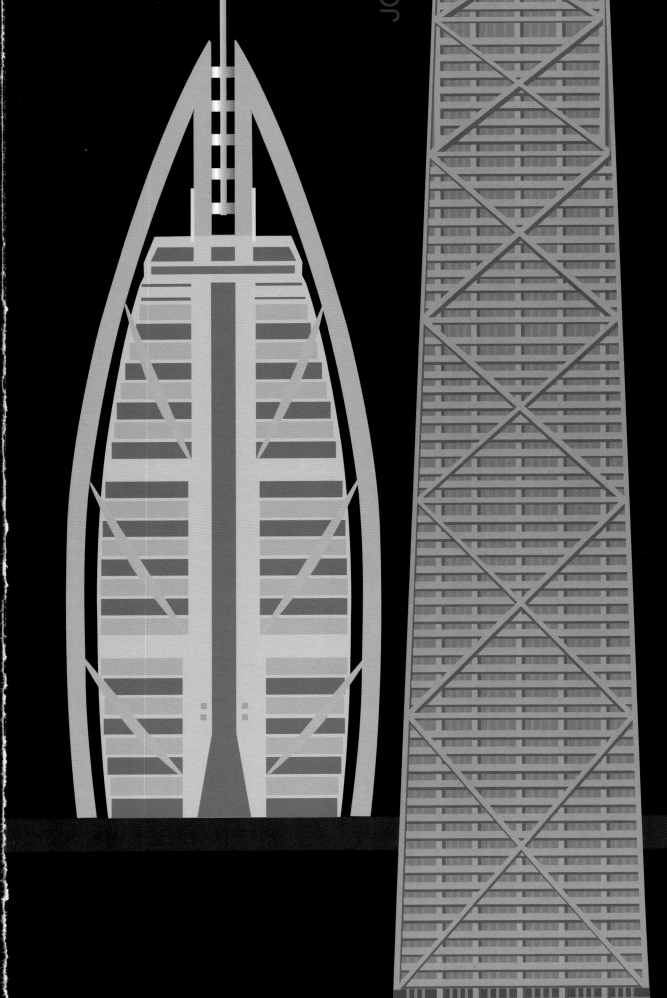

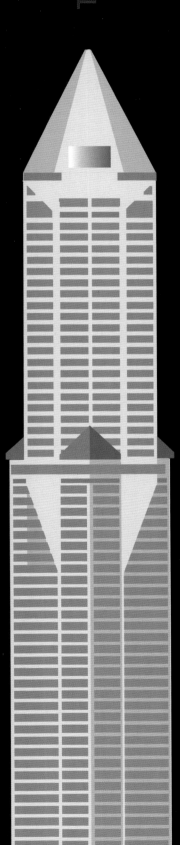

Shanghai
TOMORROW SQUARE
935 FT

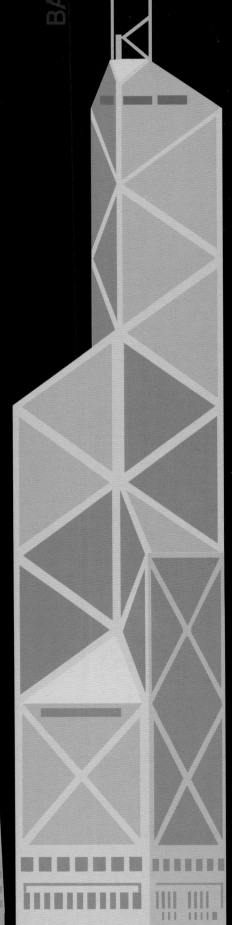

Riyadh
AL FAISALIAH CENTER
876 FT

Hong Kong
BANK OF CHINA
1,204 FT

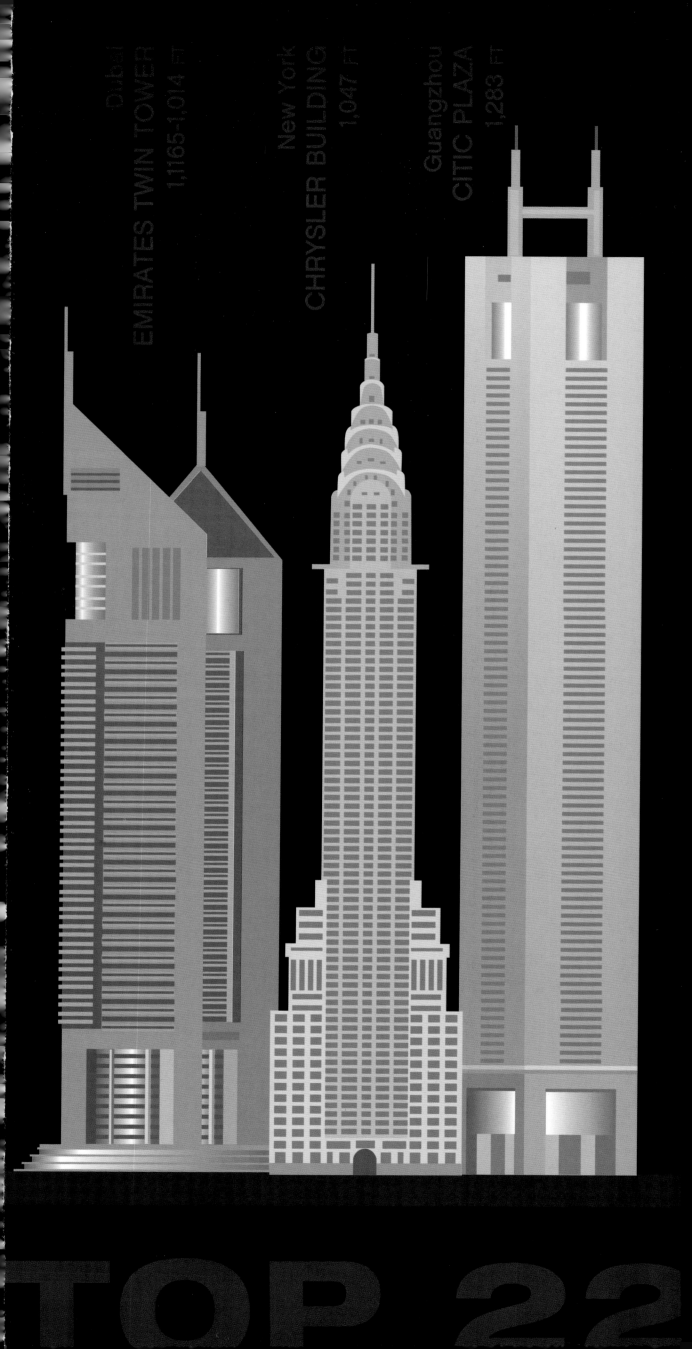

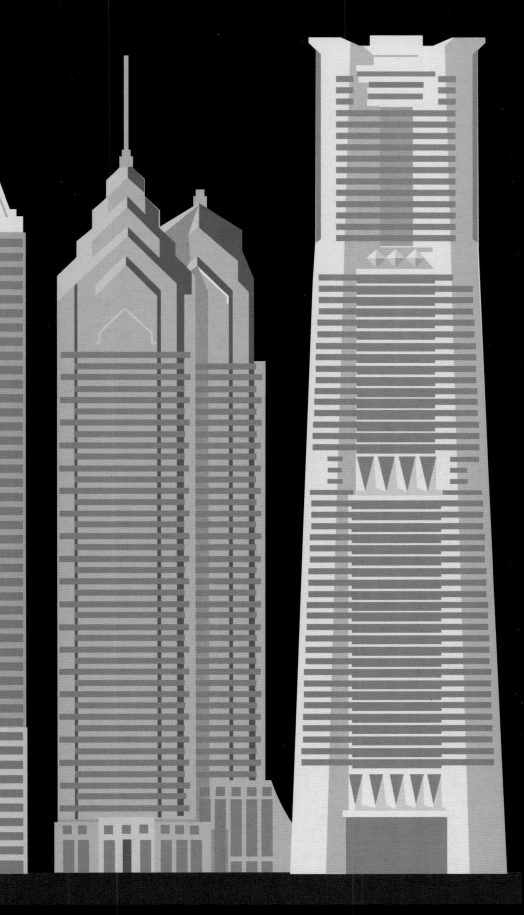

Cleveland
KEY TOWER
948 FT

Philadelphia
LIBERTY PLACE
945-847 FT

Yokohama
LANDMARK TOWER
971 FT

SKYSCRAPERS

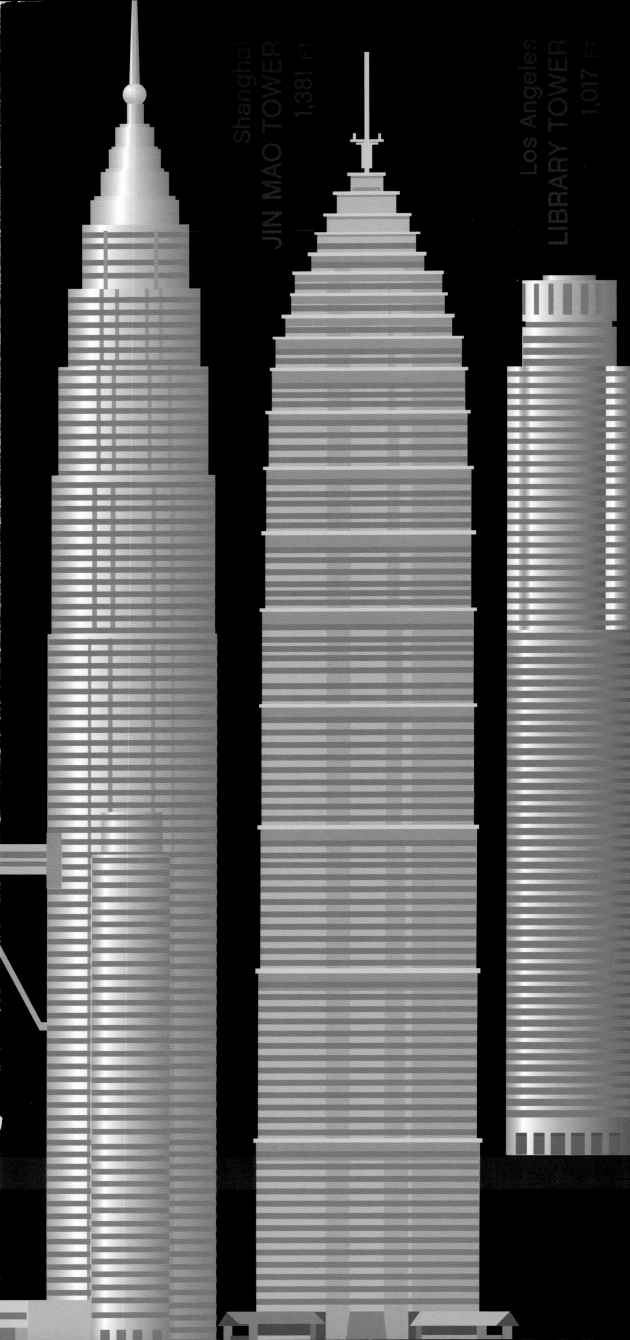

Shanghai

JIN MAO TOWER

1,381 FT

Los Angeles

LIBRARY TOWER

1,017 FT

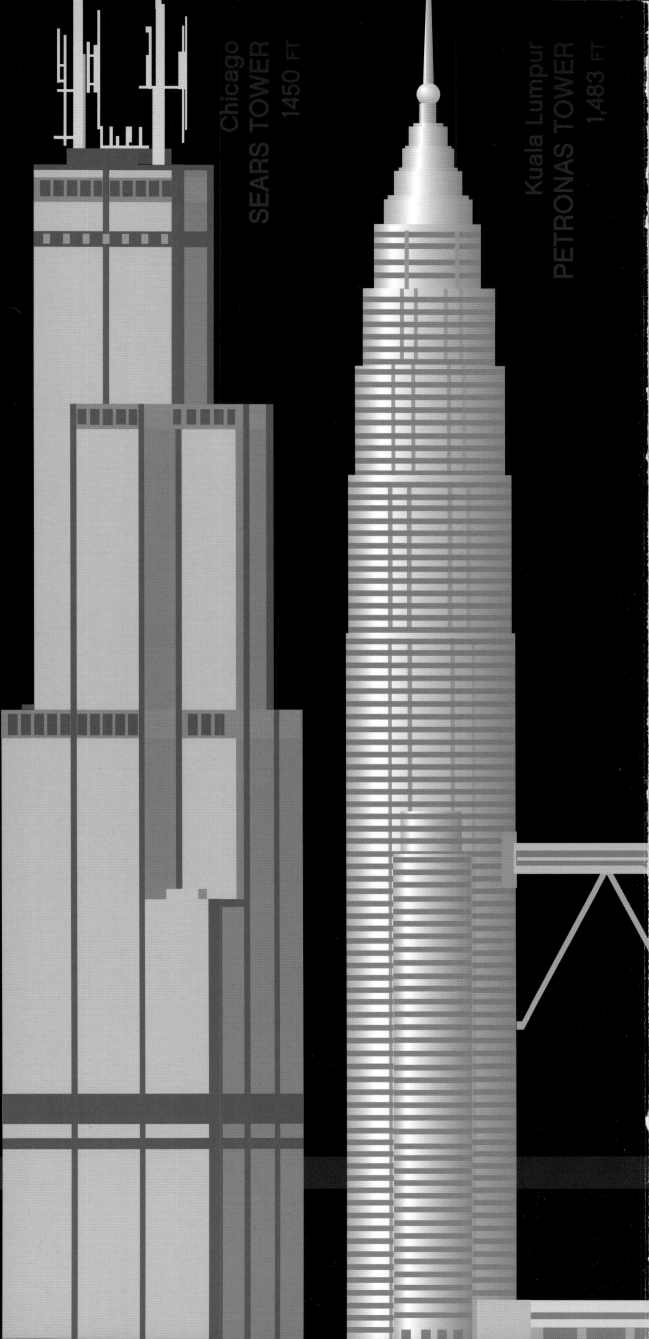

Chicago
SEARS TOWER
1450 FT

Kuala Lumpur
PETRONAS TOWER
1,483 FT

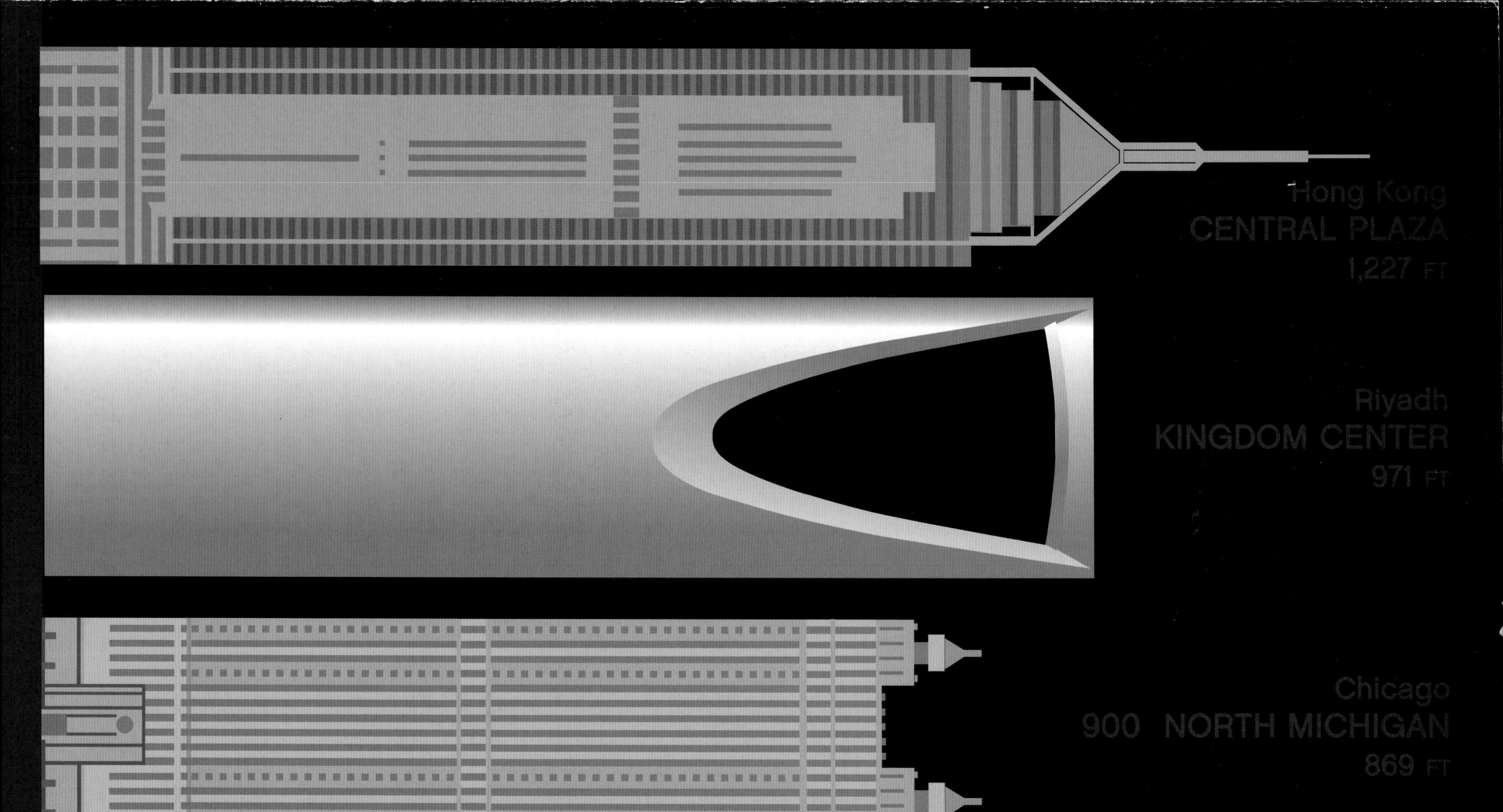

Hong Kong
CENTRAL PLAZA
1,227 FT

Riyadh
KINGDOM CENTER
971 FT

Chicago
900 NORTH MICHIGAN
869 FT